RAILWAYS OF KEITH AND DUFFTOWN

The story of the railways in Keith and the line to Dufftown

KEITH FENWICK

This is a revised and expanded version of *Railways of Keith*, published in 2006, giving more details of the line to Dufftown and bringing the story up to date.

Published by the
Great North of Scotland Railway Association

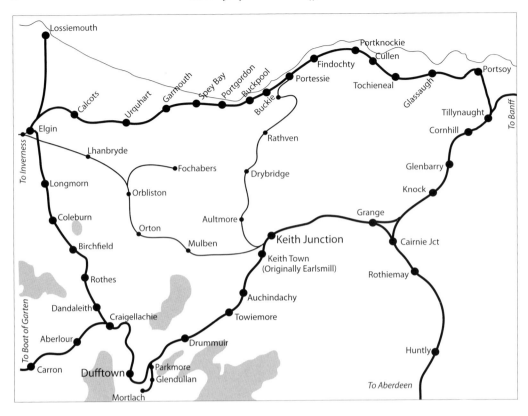

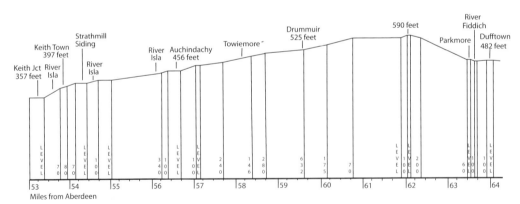

Gradient Diagram for the Keith to Dufftown section

© Keith Fenwick 2013

ISBN: 978-0902343-25-2

Published by the Great North of Scotland Railway Association, www.gnsra.org.uk

Printed by Berforts Information Press, Eynsham, Oxfordshire, OX29 4JB

Contents

Sources and Bibliography

Minute Books of the Great North of Scotland Railway, Keith & Dufftown Railway and Speyside Railway, held in the National Records of Scotland, General Register House, Edinburgh.

Great North Review and *Highland Railway Journal*, various issues.

Elgin Courant, Banffshire Journal and *Aberdeen Journal*, various issues.

Great North of Scotland Railway - A Guide, W Ferguson of Kinmundy, David Douglas, 1881

Great North of Scotland Railway (2nd Edition), H A Vallance, David St. John Thomas, 1989

History of the Great North of Scotland Railway, Sir C M Barclay-Harvey, Ian Allan.

Regional History of the Railways of Great Britain, Vol.15, J Thomas & D Turnock, David St.John Thomas, 1989

Highland Railway, David Ross, Stenlake Publishing, 2010, ISBN 9781840334975.

Highland Railway, Its Constituents and Successors, Stephenson Locomotive Society, 1955.

History of the Highland Railway, by H.A. Vallance, updated by Clinker and Lambert as *The Highland Railway*, House of Lochar, ISBN 1 899863 07 9.

LMS Engine Sheds, Volume 6, Hawkins, Reeve and Stevenson, Irwell Press, 1989, ISBN 1 871608 04X.

Speyside Railways, Rosemary Burgess & Robert Kinghorn, Aberdeen University Press, 1988

Speyside Line, a History and Guide, Keith Fenwick, Great North of Scotland Railway Association, 2012.

Traveller's Joy, the Story of the Morayshire Railway, John Ross, published by author, 2001.

Towiemore, its Railway, Lime Works and Distillery, Ron Smith, GNSRA 2009, ISBN 9780902343207.

Acknowledgements

Grateful thanks go to various members of the Great North of Scotland Railway Association, the Keith & Dufftown Railway Association and the Highland Railway Society who have helped in the preparation of this book. Particular thanks go to David Fasken for permission to use his account of the formation of the KDRA. Further details of these Societies can be found on page 64.

Thanks are also due to Ian Hird, who has contributed the chapter on his experiences at Keith in the 1960s and has created a web site www.tourofkeith.co.uk which describes the town and its environs.

The station staff at Keith pose in front of a Great North loco at Keith. The station master is the man with the top hat on the right of the main group. The Dufftown platform is on the left. Behind can be seen the original overall roof, which seems to be showing its age. It was removed in the 1920s and replaced by platform awnings.

(GNSR Association)

The west end of Keith about 1912, showing the other end of the overall roof. The original plan was that the platforms under the main roof would be used for the line to Elgin, but instead a new platform was built on the north side (left in this view) and the roof extended to cover it. In the centre is the bay later provided for Buckie trains and on the right the end of the siding which served the Highland goods shed. On the far left, coaches are parked on the loop behind the through platform.

(GNSR Association)

Introduction

Keith was for many years an important railway town. The first line reached there in 1856; two years later it became the frontier between the two companies which provided the through route between Aberdeen and Inverness but who did not always get on well with each other. The branch to Dufftown was opened in 1862 and the following year it was extended to Speyside and was also linked up with the Morayshire Railway to Elgin.

The first line was the Great North of Scotland Railway's extension from Huntly; formally opened on 10th October 1856, regular services started the following day. It was originally intended that the GNSR would build the railway all the way to Inverness, but finance proved a problem. Instead, the route was completed by the Inverness & Aberdeen Junction Railway, later part of the Highland Railway, and so Keith became the exchange point between the two companies.

Although this restricted the development of through services between Aberdeen and Inverness, Keith was all the more important in railway terms. Both companies established locomotive sheds there and employed a large staff to handle the interchange of traffic.

Once the line to Keith had opened, local interests promoted a branch to Portsoy and Banff, connecting at Grange with the main line, and another to Dufftown. The GNSR came to the rescue of the latter when it could not raise enough capital so that it could be part of a route down Speyside. Connection was also made at Craigellachie with the Morayshire Railway, creating an alternative route to Elgin.

In the 1880s, when the fishing industry expanded, the Highland built a line over the hills to Buckie, but that was never really successful and it was closed as an economy measure during the First World War.

Keith continued to be an important railway town well into the 20th century. It remained an interchange point between the LNER and LMS railways between the Wars. Even after British Railways was formed, previous operational practices continued. The facilities were gradually run down during the 1950s and 1960s, as much of the traffic was lost by the railways and steam was replaced by diesel traction. The passenger service was revolutionised in 1960 with the introduction of through fast diesel trains between Aberdeen and Inverness. This formed the basis of an enhanced through service when the passenger facilities via Dufftown were withdrawn in 1968.

The Dufftown branch struggled on for a few years carrying freight, latterly just coal to Dufftown. Local enterprise, in the form of Grampian Railtours, led the way to revival by the use of the line for tourist excursions and these kept it going for several more years. When they eventually ceased, the Keith & Dufftown Railway Association came to the rescue. It is now one of the tourist attractions of the area.

Keith continues to be an important stop on the Aberdeen to Inverness service. Hopefully the next few years will see some much needed investment to ensure its continued popularity.

With two stations in Keith, it is sometimes not clear which is which. In this book, Keith refers to the Junction station. The other station is always referred to as Keith Town, or in its earlier guise, as Earlsmill.

Huntly station from the north end, showing the overall roof which dated from the opening of the station. This was easily adapted as a through station when the line was extended. The goods yard was behind the left platform at the other end of the station. The small signal box shown here was opened in 1890 to control the north end of the loop. It was replaced by Huntly Station box at the other end of the platforms in 1901.

(GNSR Association)

Two viaducts over the Deveron sat side by side at Rothiemay for many years. The original viaduct, with its remarkably skewed arches, is on the right; remained until the 1970s when it was taken down due to its condition. The replacement, built when the line was doubled in 1900, is on the left. *(GNSR Association)*

The Line from Huntly

The first railway to Keith was proposed during the railway mania of the mid-1840s when the Great North of Scotland Railway was promoted by commercial interests in Aberdeen to run to Inverness by way of Inverurie, Huntly, Keith and Elgin. This scheme was not supported by people in Inverness who wanted control of the railway serving their town and, in any case, preferred a direct route to the south via Druimuachdar.

There was also an argument about the best route northwards from Aberdeen, as the GNSR route missed the important town of Banff. This led to an alternative proposal, the Aberdeen, Banff & Elgin Railway, which would have left Keith to be served by a 10 or 15 mile branch from the coast.

These proposals came before Parliament in 1846. The direct line from Perth to Inverness was rejected because of its steep gradients and the line to Elgin via Banff because its promoters could not prove that it had enough genuine financial support.

The Great North of Scotland Railway was incorporated in August 1846 and authorised to build a double track main line to Inverness, along with three branches, at a total estimated cost of £1,500,000. By then, the railway mania was over and finance could not be raised, especially where such a large amount was involved.

Over the next few years the GNSR continued pursuing its objective and eventually, in 1852, raised enough capital to start construction of a single track line from Kittybrewster, on the northern edge of Aberdeen, to Huntly. This was opened in September 1854, by which time the company's powers to build any more of the line had lapsed.

The people in Inverness now had their opportunity and started building eastward, initially only as far as Nairn as that town was common to both the Aberdeen and Perth routes to the south. Moreover, it was an easy line to build, 18 miles across flat ground. The Inverness & Nairn was authorised in 1854 and opened in November 1855.

Huntly was only a temporary terminus; the GNSR still aimed to continue towards Inverness. Discussions were held with the I&N, who wanted to extend to Elgin but the GNSR was concerned that it would then be left to build the relatively expensive section between Keith and Elgin. The half-way point was roughly where the Spey would be crossed at Boat of Brig and an agreement was initially reached that both companies would build to that point. On further consideration, it was realised that the bridge over the Spey was not the best place for two companies to meet, so it was decided that the line from Nairn would extend to Keith and that the GNSR would pay for the section from Keith to the Spey, as well as extending its line from Huntly.

The GNSR promoted a Bill in the 1854/55 session to construct its line to Keith. There does not seem to have been much opposition to this. The Great North of Scotland Railway Extension Act was duly passed on 25th May 1855. The estimated cost of the extension was £80,000 and work commenced soon after the Act was passed.

The line from Huntly follows the River Deveron, initially on its eastern bank. At Rothiemay the river was crossed on a magnificent five arch skew viaduct, 70 feet high. Colonel Wynne, who inspected the line for the Board of Trade, said that it was one of the best pieces of work he had inspected and was built on the greatest skew he had seen. At Rothiemay a station was provided on the west bank and then the line followed the course of the River Isla to Keith. A second intermediate station was opened at Grange on 5th January 1857.

The terminus at Keith was described in the *Banffshire Journal* (14th October 1856) as "an extensive affair. The principal landing place measures in length 166 feet and is 60 feet wide. A carriage-shed attached to the north side of the station is 250 feet in length. The accommodation for goods is ample; the station for this portion of the traffic measuring 112 feet by 28. The engine house is 100 feet by 30. Refreshment rooms, 40 feet long, are being erected. A very handsome building is nearly completed for the residence of the station-master, who, by the way, is Mr. Bruce, who since the opening of the line so efficiently discharged the same duties at Huntly. The whole contract for the station buildings here was taken by Mr Brand. The joiner work was done under his own eye, but the mason work was executed for him by Messrs Greig, Aberdeen; the slater work by Mr Keith, Aberdeen; the plumber work by a Montrose firm; and the plaster work by Mr Falconer, Forres. The work is exceedingly well done. The station is closed at the west end. The whole of the fittings, however, are so arranged that they can easily be removed so as to form an open front when the time comes for opening up the Inverness Junction." Gas lighting was provided at that time, as the GNSR Minutes of 16th September 1856 noted that gas had been connected to Keith station.

The proceedings on 10th October began with a special train over the new line. Stations were elaborately decorated with flowers, triumphal arches, etc., and even private houses were ornamented with flags of all kinds. At Rothiemay, the passengers got out to admire the viaduct.

The inhabitants of Keith invited the directors and officers to dine with them and in due time upwards of two hundred were comfortably seated in the "commodious and tastefully ornamented shed in connection with the station".

The only intermediate station on the opening of the extension to Keith was at Rothiemay, Early maps show it with three sidings behind the up platform but the station was rebuilt and the platforms realigned when the new bridge over the Deveron was built for the doubling of the line. This is the station, from the north end, on its last day of service in May 1968, very rundown as it had been unstaffed for several years. (Keith Fenwick)

Grange was opened early in 1857. This postcard view dates from the 1920s or early 1930s. The line to Keith is to the left. Everything is neat and tidy. Trains for Portsoy and Banff used the bay platform behind the footbridge but this fell out of use after the opening of the Coast line. Today nothing is left apart from a single track and the overgrown remains of the platforms. (J Cruickshank)

The chair was occupied by the Hon. T C Bruce, Commissioner for the Earl of Seafield. The principal guests were the GNSR chairman, Sir James Elphinstone, and four other GNSR directors plus Alexander Gibb, their Engineer, and Robert Milne, General Manager. Bruce proposed the toast to "The Directors of the Great North" and congratulated them on the completion of their works so far. He complimented especially the Duke of Richmond and Sir James Elphinstone for the support they had shown. Referring to railways generally, he said that there had been a change over the previous few years; immense returns were no longer expected. If they wanted the railway system extended, "we must put our own shoulders to the wheel and help ourselves".

In reply, Sir James told how they had carried on after 1850. In that year, the undertaking had been in a manner abandoned. The principal person in this resuscitation was the Duke of Richmond, who guaranteed £15,000. Sir James had given a year's rent of his estates in guarantee, and Mr Morison of Bognie had done the same. This enabled the raising of the necessary capital.

Among the other toasts of the evening was success to the Inverness & Nairn Railway, replied to by Andrew Dougall, its Manager. He noted that 40 miles remained to link the two railways but that distance did not prevent a mutual and friendly understanding between them and he hoped it might long continue. Several other toasts followed, before the company, warned "by the impatient screams of the engine", broke up and returned home.

The bonhomie between the GNSR and I&N was perhaps the high point of their relationship in the nineteenth century. Over the next few years, mutual distrust grew and there was a noticeable lack of cooperation. Bruce and his employer, the Earl of Seafield, were very much involved with the I&N and its successors; Bruce later became chairman of the Highland Railway. With his local connections, he was before that chairman of the Banff, Portsoy & Strathisla Railway, which built the branches to Portsoy and Banff and was later absorbed by the GNSR.

GNSR Class 1 No.7 was delivered in December 1854 from Fairbairn & Co, Manchester. It was the last of this class which was built for the opening of the line to Huntly. By the time the line was extended to Keith, five more locos of similar design but known as Class 8 were also in service. This photo shows No.7 as rebuilt with a rudimentary cab. It only survived a few years before it was withdrawn in 1900.   (GNSR Association)

The Highland Railway's entrance to Keith, as seen from the end of the platform. The locomotive shed is in the centre, by this time accommodating a few spare horse boxes, and the bay platform built for Buckie trains to the left behind the photographer. The Highland's turntable can be seen on the far right. The Buckie branch went off to the right into the hills just beyond the West signal box which can be seen in the distance. This photo was taken before 1951, by which time the roof of the shed had disappeared.

(Graham Maxtone collection)

Through to Elgin and Inverness

Even as the GNSR opening to Keith was being celebrated, preparations were under way to begin construction of the line westwards. The *Inverness Courier* reported on 23rd October 1856 that the contractors, Messrs Mitchell, Dean & Co. were in a position to start work.

The Inverness & Aberdeen Junction Railway was incorporated by Act of Parliament on 21st July 1856 to build the line from Nairn to Keith. Although nominally a separate company from the I&N to keep the finances apart, both companies shared the same management and were operated as one. The capital of the I&AJ was £325,000, of which £40,000 was subscribed by the GNSR to pay for the section from Keith to the Spey crossing. The GNSR was also to appoint two directors to the I&AJ Board and a joint station was to be set up at Keith.

Construction of the line involved two significant river crossings. As well as the Spey at Boat of Brig, the Findhorn was crossed just to the west of Forres. It was not until 25th March 1858 that the line was opened to Elgin from the west. The Spey Bridge took much longer and, as often happened, the I&AJ was so short of capital that it had to cut corners. It was anxious to get the line opened during the summer of 1858 and erected a temporary structure about which the Board of Trade was very unhappy. Their inspector paid several visits and grew impatient with the company, firstly for inviting him before the line was anywhere near ready and then for wanting to run passenger trains over the temporary bridge.

Eventually, he agreed to the opening of the line except for the Spey Crossing. Passengers would have to detrain and either walk across the adjacent road bridge or be conveyed by bus. This opening took place on 18th August 1858, thus completing the through route from Inverness to Aberdeen. Early timetables showed an extra 15 minutes for the crossing of the River Spey, but that disappeared early the following year. Exactly when the Spey Bridge opened fully is unclear; the I&AJ started using it without permission from the Board of Trade. A half-hearted enquiry was carried out during 1859, but the BoT Inspector seems to have decided not to challenge the *fait accompli.* That would never happen these days!

It might have been thought that, once the through route was open, the GNSR and the I&AJ would settle down to work in harmony. Far from it. The GNSR directors on the I&AJ board do not seem to have taken any part in the management of that company but confined themselves to asking awkward questions, even if these were aimed at identifying dubious practices on the part of the I&AJ. By 1860, relations were so strained that the GNSR gave up all involvement with the I&AJ and its shares in the company were sold to some of the I&AJ directors.

To accommodate the I&AJ, a new platform was built on the north side of the original platforms where there had originally been a lean-to to store carriages, although the buildings had been designed so that the central portion could be opened up at the west end. Perhaps it was thought preferable to keep the trains of the two companies apart. Only one platform was provided for Elgin trains, with a loop to enable I&AJ locomotives to run round the trains and reach the turntable at the west end of the station. The Great North continued to operate the station under its Agent with the I&AJ paying a rent for the use of its passenger and goods facilities. The I&AJ built its own 4-road locomotive shed at the west end. The GNSR Agent eventually controlled a large number of Highland staff. Some enhancements, such as the addition in 1874 of a crane for weighing dead meat, were paid for jointly.

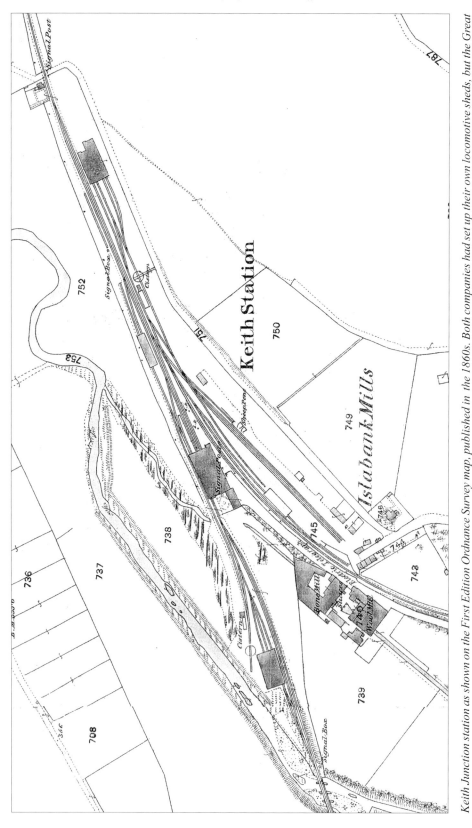

Keith Junction station as shown on the First Edition Ordnance Survey map, published in the 1860s. Both companies had set up their own locomotive sheds, but the Great North's passenger and goods facilities were used for all the traffic. The goods shed is just below the main passenger building. The shed on the north side of the line at the east end was for carriage storage; one track was provided for each company but there was no connection between them. The track alignment in both the Huntly and Elgin directions would have easily suited a straight run through the station. (Reproduced with permission of the Ordnance Survey.)

Keith and Dufftown Railway

The original proposal for a line to Dufftown was made by local parties, some of whom had been involved in promoting the line from Grange to Banff and Portsoy. The Keith & Dufftown Railway Minutes record that the first meeting took place at the Fife Arms Hotel in Dufftown Square on 21st October 1856 attended by James Petrie, Bank Agent in Dufftown; James Findlater, Factor for the Earl of Fife; William Cantlie, of Keithmore; and Mr Falconer. The GNSR, which was developing various other branches at that time, offered to work the line.

The line as originally planned started from a junction with the I&AJ near a farm called Strypeside some distance from Keith and terminated in a field on the farm of Parkbeg, close to where the Boharn road joined the Botriphnie turnpike; that is over a mile from Dufftown. Judging by the statements made at one its meetings, the I&AJ does not seem to have been consulted about the proposed junction with the Dufftown line.

Finance was always a problem for the K&D. To comply with Parliamentary Standing Orders, the promoters should have secured *bona fide* subscribers for all the proposed shares and obtained a deposit of 10% on each of them. Subscribers came forward for only £13,470 worth of shares; agents signed for the rest. With this way of getting round the rules, the promoters obtained their Act and the Company was incorporated on 27th July 1857 with a capital of £50,000.

It still proved impossible to sell the shares and no progress was made on construction. After what must have been a lot of behind the scenes activity, the Great North came to the rescue in 1859. It undertook to provide up to half the capital, provided the rest was raised locally. The route was altered to start from Keith station and a new Act was obtained, the Keith & Dufftown Railway (Deviation) Act, on 25th May 1860. The Dufftown terminus was moved a bit closer to the town, to a point 177 yards on the north side of the road leading to the farmhouses of Little Tulloch, not far from the present Parkmore quarry and the Fiddich viaduct. The Great North now took an active part in the management of the company and appointed five directors.

Construction started later in 1860. Most of the route was relatively easy, with no major bridges but several earthworks. In June 1860, the company agreed that they would avoid taking down the castle at Keith, on promise of £25 subscriptions from the people of Keith and liberal dealing on land settlement from the Seafield estate to cover the additional cost.

The contractor was Brand & Sons, who were to be paid £24,000 if the line was complete by 1st August 1861 or £24,607 if completed two months earlier. By then the Company had decided that the terminus should be at Balvenie, closer to the town but still over half a mile away.

Events far away now took a hand in the affairs of the K&D with the promotion of the line from Forres to Perth via Grantown and Kingussie, effectively by the I&AJ. A direct route over the hills from Inverness to the south had long been the ambition of the people of Inverness but its promotion, so soon after completion of the Inverness to Aberdeen route, was partly as a result of the difficulties of travelling via Aberdeen for which the GNSR was largely blamed. Not only did the connection at Aberdeen involve a half mile journey between stations but the GNSR was in the habit of failing to connect with late-running trains from the south.

The GNSR stood to lose significant revenue once the Perth line was opened and came up with a rival proposal to serve the relatively prosperous upper Spey valley around Grantown

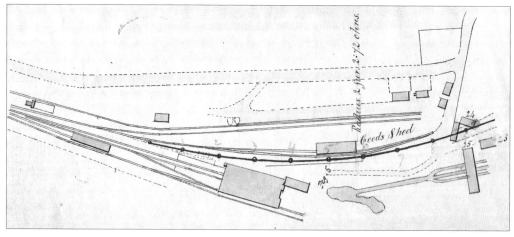

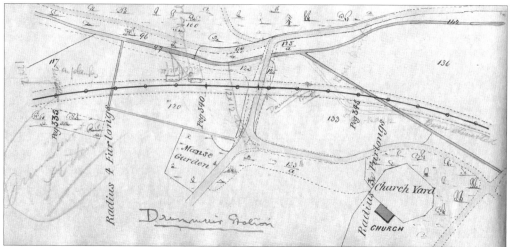

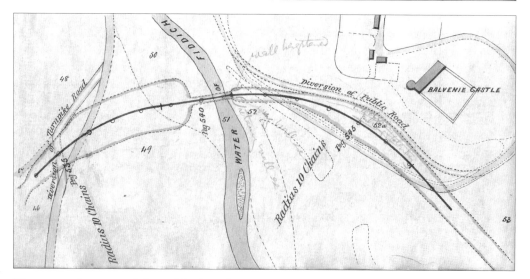

Three pages from a set of plans of the branch which include the Balvenie Extension showing Keith (top), Drummuir (middle) and Dufftown (bottom).   *(Courtesy Mike Stephen)*

by proposing a line from Dufftown via Craigellachie to Grantown and Abernethy. Lucrative timber traffic in the upper Spey area around Grantown was anticipated; the GNSR ignored the fact that this was mainly on Seafield land and that the Earl was a committed supporter of the railways based in Inverness.

The route of the GNSR line, to be called the Speyside Railway, carried on from the K&D over the Fiddich, northwards to Craigellachie and then up the Spey Valley. Aberlour and Grantown were the only significant places served; parts of the valley were sparsely populated in those days as the whisky industry had hardly been developed.

Meanwhile, the K&D took steps to construct the extension to Balvenie in advance of obtaining parliamentary powers. A contract for the extra work was agreed for £12,723 in October as a normal part of the preparation of the parliamentary Bill, but the contract was on the understanding that it was completed in the same timescale as the main contract, i.e. by August, 1861. Power to build the extension was included in the Strathspey Railway Act (17th May 1861) and this saved the cost of a separate Act but was later to cause problems with the Company's accounts.

By April 1861, tenders were agreed for the following :

Keith [Town]   station house £93.5.0

Towie   station house £220.6.0, goods shed £106.5.6

Drummuir   station house £233.16.6, goods shed £106.8.0

Dufftown   station house £323, goods shed £127.17.0, carriage shed £136. engine shed £116.

There were complaints in May that not enough progress was being made. At that time Brand employed 460 labourers, 83 masons, 60 quarry men, 6 joiners, 6 blacksmiths and 60 horses; the Engineer wanted an extra 150 labourers, 30 masons, 5 joiners and 10 horses. In June, tenders were agreed for Pointsmen and Weighbridge boxes and Choke Blocks for stations on the line for a total of £43.16.0. Other smaller items included 8 distant semaphore signals, 1 disc signal,

The two arches of the Fiddich viaduct as seen from the field to the south in 1989. Over the years, the trees have gradually encroached on the viaduct. (Keith Fenwick)

5 switch signals and the removal of 1 disc signal from Aberdeen to Keith at a cost of £215.12.0 and the supply and fitting of a cast iron water tank at Dufftown for £85.

The opening depended on completion of the Fiddich Viaduct. This was a substantial structure consisting of two arches of brick resting on granite buttresses at either side and a strong pillar of granite in the centre of the river. The elevation of the arches was fifty feet above the level of the water and between them they spanned a distance of 132 feet. Construction of the line was well advanced in early summer, with opening expected in August when, on 9th July, the centre pier collapsed, bringing down the rest of the structure. The accident happened while the 34 men employed on the bridge were at breakfast; providentially, the foreman thinking his watch was slow, had put it forward 5 minutes the previous day otherwise they would have been on the bridge at the time it collapsed.

Sadly, the 11-year old daughter of a labourer, William Robertson of Botriphnie, had brought his breakfast to him and the two of them took shelter under one of the arches. They were killed instantly by the collapse. It took the workmen until 7am the next morning to clear the rubble and recover the bodies.

Rebuilding commenced almost immediately, but with the centre pillar in granite ashlar throughout at an extra cost of £62.12.0.

The number of men employed continued to cause concern. Only 70 additional men were at work in June; by July there was a total of 799 but this had fallen to 507 in September when, no doubt, harvesting would take some away. The Engineer thought that if 300 more were employed the line could be completed by the end of October.

By November 1861 track was laid from Keith nearly to the Fiddich viaduct. Rails for the sidings at Botriphnie, Drummuir and Dufftown were laid and station houses and goods

Dufftown station from the hill to the south. The line from Keith comes in from the right and then heads north towards Craigellachie. The distillery in the foreground is now Glenfiddich, while Balvenie is near the centre, to the right of the line. The station yard is full of wagons.   (George Washington Wilson)

This photograph from the early 1960s, should show a railbus on its way to Aviemore, but it had failed and a Type 2 loco hauling one coach deputised for it. It is seen in the sylvan setting of Drummuir in the 1960s. The village is up the hill to the right, while the train will shortly pass Loch Park. The goods yard can be seen to the right of the station building. (Graham Maxtone collection)

sheds nearly finished. By February, the line was complete. Goods services started on 19th February.

Two separate Board of Trade inspections were involved. On February 19th, Colonel Rich reported that he had inspected a single line, 9 miles 1 chain, from Keith to near Dufftown that day. There was a siding near Keith. The switches were of ordinary construction with double rods. There were no level crossings. An engine turntable had been constructed at Keith. There were stations at Earlsmill, half a mile from Keith, Botriphnie 3 miles 3 furlongs and Drummuir 6 miles 2½ furlongs. A satisfactory certificate as to the mode of working accompanied the report and sanction to open was recommended.

The following day, Colonel Rich reported inspecting the portion of the Strathspey Railway extending from Little Tulloch to Balvenie, Little Tulloch being the place where the Keith & Dufftown Railway ended and the Strathspey Railway commenced. The length of the latter to its existing terminus at Balvenie, now called Dufftown Street (sic), was 1 mile 53 chains. The line was single throughout with sidings at Dufftown station. Patent switches with double connecting rods were used on the line. An engine turntable was provided at Dufftown and indicators were attached to the facing points. There were two over and one under bridges, the latter having masonry abutments and cast iron girders. The other two bridges had brick arches and masonry abutments. The spans were 17ft, 25ft and 12ft. The bridges were well built and of sufficient strength for the requirements of the line. There were three viaducts, two of small span having masonry abutments and cast iron girders. The third called Fiddick (sic) Viaduct consisted of two segmental brick arches of 62ft span which rose 50ft above the bed of the river. The whole were well built and of sufficient strength. The line approached this viaduct from Little Tulloch on a falling gradient of 1 in 60 and the curve at the bottom of the gradient was

GREAT NORTH OF SCOTLAND RAILWAY.

OPENING FOR TRAFFIC—KEITH AND DUFFTOWN SECTION.

ON FRIDAY, 21st February, 1862, and until further Notice, TRAINS will be worked between KEITH and DUFFTOWN in connection with the Main Line and Branches as under:—

DOWN TRAINS Will not Depart from	1 Class 1 and 3	2 Class 1 and 3	3 Class 1 and 2 Parl.	4 Class 1 and 3	UP TRAINS Will not depart from	1 Class 1 and 3	2 Class 1 and 3 Parl.	3 Class 1 and 3	4 Class 1 and 3
	A.M.	A.M.	A.M.	P.M.		A.M.	A.M.	P.M.	P.M.
ABERDEEN before	—	8 0	11 0	4 40	DUFFTOWN before	6 0	9 10	12 30	5 25
OLD DEER and MINTLAW..	—	—	7 20	11 30a	DRUMMUIR	6 20	9 26	12 46	5 40
DYCE JUNCTION	8 26	11 29	6 2		BOTRIPHNIE	6 35	9 36	12 56	5 50
ALFORD	—	7 40	10 45	2 30	EARLSMILL	—	—	—	—
KINTORE	—	8 54	11 50	5 22	KEITH arrive	6 50	9 50	1 10	6 4
OLDMELDRUM	—	8 24	11 30	2 55	Do. depart	7 0	10 5	1 20	6 15
INVERURY	—	9 3	12 5	5 32					
BANFF and MACDUFF ...	—	6 50	10 0	1 0	Elgin, per I. & A. Jun..	8 0	12 7	—	8 43
INVERAMSAY	—	9 15	12 17	5 44	Inverness, arrive......	9 50	1 45	—	10 15
HUNTLY	—	10 21	1 28	6 47					
					GRANGE depart	7 11	10 20	1 33	6 26
Banff, per B. P. & S....	—	9 15	12 35	5 0					
Portsoy, "	—	9 27	12 40	5 14	Banff, per B. P. & S...ar.	—	11 45	3 5	8 0
					Portsoy, " "	—	11 50	3 15	8 10
GRANGE	—	10 40	1 54	7 8					
					HUNTLY .....dep.	7 33	10 46	1 57	6 47
Inverness, per I. & A. Jun.	—	6 40	10 15	3 15	INVERAMSAY	8 32	11 54	2 7	7 50
Elgin, ...	—	8 3	12 10	5 11	BANFF and MACDUFF ar.	11 10	2 10	—	9 50
					INVERURY .....dep.	8 32	12 5	3 17	8 3
KEITH arrive	—	10 51	2 5	7 20	OLDMELDRUM ......ar.	9 25	12 25	—	8 25
Do. depart	8 0	11 0	2 15	7 30	KINTORE ....dep.	8 54	12 15	3 25	8 12
EARLSMILL	—	—	—	—.	ALFORD ....ar.	10 5	1 20	—	9 10
BOTRIPHNIE	8 14	11 20	2 30	7 45	DYCE JUNCTION......dep.	9 16	12 39	3 47	8 33
DRUMMUIR	8 24	11 35	2 40	7 55	OLD DEER & MINTLAW.ar.	10 50	2 50	6 0	—
DUFFTOWN arrive	8 40	11 50	2 50	8 10	ABERDEEN	9 45	1 5	4 20	9 0

" Classes " of Trains refer only to Great North of Scotland Line and Branches.

For Passenger Fares, Conditions under which Tickets are issued, Goods Trains, &c. &c., see Great North of Scotland Railway Company's Time Tables.

The Agents at the respective Stations will give Information as to Rates for the conveyance of Goods, Live Stock, &c. &c.

By Order,

ROBERT MILNE, GENERAL MANAGER.

Aberdeen, 19th February, 1862.

one of 10 chains. A third guard rail was laid all along the way round the curve and over the viaduct. Nevertheless it was a place which should be approached at a very moderate speed. The embankment on the south side of the line at about 45 chains from its commencement up to 60 chains was washed by a small but rapid stream. A small portion at the foot of the embankment had been piled and sheeted to prevent the slope from giving way. This piling and sheeting required to be continued for the whole distance. Col Rich enclosed an undertaking from the Engineer of the Company to execute this work within three months from the date of the inspection and also to remove a second set of facing points then placed at the approach to Dufftown station.

This enabled passenger services to start the following day, Friday 21st February. The people of Dufftown marked it with a holiday.

The initial timetable, reproduced here from the *Peterhead Sentinel*, shows four trains each way daily, taking between 35 and 50 minutes for the 10½ mile journey. Earlsmill, the name by which Keith Town was known until 1 May 1897, was not ready but was opened later in the year. As often happened with new lines, traffic in the first few months was buoyant, the more so at Dufftown as it was the railhead for the construction material for the Strathspey line, as illustrated in the extract from the *Banffshire Journal* on page 21. This allowed the directors to declare a dividend of 1½% later that year and give optimistic predictions of prosperity to come. As early as 7th March 1862 Mr Innes of Aberlour was running a bus service to Dufftown to connect with train services.

The Strathspey Railway was proceeding and on 1st July 1863 the line was extended from

INVERNESS AND PERTH AND INVERNESS AND ABERDEEN JUNCTION RAILWAYS.

OPENING OF THE INVERNESS AND PERTH LINE THROUGHOUT.

ON 1st DECEMBER 1863, and until further notice, the Trains will Arrive and Depart at the following Hours, or as near thereto as circumstances will permit, viz. :—

Time taken from the Railway Clocks.

Up Trains.

STATIONS.	1 Pass. Mail Class 1 & 3	2 Par. Class 1 & 3	3 Parl. Class 1 & 3	4 Pass. Class 1 & 3	5 Pass. Class 1 & 3	6 Pass. Class 1 & 3	7 Pass. Class 1 & 3	Sunday Trains. 1 Parl. Mail	2 Parl. Mail
Coaches leave				A.M.		A.M.	noon		
Thurso, ...	12 0						12 0		
Wick, ...	4 6p						4 6p		
Golspie, ...	11·55						11 30	11 55	
	A.M.						P.M.	A.M.	
Tain, ...	3 19				9 30		4 41	3 19	
Trains leave	A.M.	A.M.	A.M.	A.M.	A.M.	P.M.	P.M.	A.M.	A.M.
Invergordon,	4 50	8·9			11 10		4 0	4 50	
Alness, ...	4 59	8 10			11 19		4 8	4 59	
Novar, ...	5 9	8 20			11 28		4 17	5 9	
Fowlis, ...		8 28			11 37		4 24		
Dingwall,	5 24	8 40			11 48		4 37	5 24	
Conon, ...	5 31	8 50			11 55		4 44	5 31	
Muir of Ord,	5 41	9 0			12 3p		4 52	5 41	
Beauly, ...	5 51	9 10			12 11		5 2	5 51	
Clunes, ...		9 17			12 17		5 8		
Lentran, ...	6 3	9 22			12 23		5 13	6 3	
Bunchrew,		9 28			12 30		5 19		
Arrive at									
Inverness,	6 20	9 40			12 40		5 30	6 20	
Leave			Mix.	Exp.					
Inverness,	6 40		*8 0	10 2	*1 5	3 5	6 20	6 40	8 0
Culloden,			8 10	10 35	1 15	3 14	6 30		8 10
Dalcross,...			8 20	10 50	1 25	3 22	6 42		8 20
Fort-George,	7 0		8 39	11 10	1 32	3 29	6 50	7 2	8 30
Nairn, ...	7 13		8 45	11 40	1 47	3 42	7 6	7 15	8 45
Brodie, ...	7 25		9 0	11 55	2 2	3 58	7 20	7 27	9 0
Arrive at									
Forres	7 35		9 15	12 15	2 10	4 5	7 30	7 35	9 15
Leave				Pass			Mail.		
Keith, ...			7 45	11 9	12 35	4 15	7 30		
Mulben, ...			8 1	11 15	12 50	4 28	7 45		
Orton, ...			8 12	11 26	1 2	4 39	7 56		
Fochabers,			8 21	11 34	1 12	4 47	8 5		
Lhanbryde,			8 34	11 42	1 21	4 55	8 15		
Elgin, ...			8 45	11 52	1 30	5 5	8 30		
Alves, ...			8 58	12 7p	1 45	5 25	8 45		
Burghd. { ar.			9 20	12 30	2 20	5 58			
{ de.			7 30	11 45	1 20	4 20			
				A.M.					
Kinloss, ,,			9 7	12 18	1 57	5 43	9 0		
Findhrn { ar.			9 53	1 5	2 18	6 48			
{ de			8 45	11 55	1 30	5 20			
Arrive				A.M.					
Forres			9 15	12 25	2 5	5 55	9 8		
Leave	Pass.					Mix.			
Forres, ...			9 20		2 15	4 45			9 20
Rafford, ...			9 30			5 0			9 38
Dunphail,			9 47		2 38	5 27			9 49
Grantown,			10 33		3 12	6 20			10 33
Broomhill,			10 45			6 35			10 45
Boat of Garten,			10 55		3 28	6 55			10 55
Aviemore,			11 10			7 15			11 10
Boat of Insh,			11 26			7 40			11 26
Kingussie,			11 45		4 5	8 0			11 45
Newtonmore,			11 55						11 55
			P.M.						P.M.
Dalwhinnie,			12 25		4 37				12 25
Struan, ...			1 20		5 22				1 20
Blair-Athole,	7 50	11 30	1 34		5 35				1 34
Pitlochry,	8 10	11 47	1 52		5 52				1 52
Ballinluig,	8 25	12 0	2 6		6 3				2 6
Guay, ...	8 30	12 7p	2 16						2 16
Dalguise,	8 35	12 12	2 22		6 11				2 22
Dunkeld,...	8 50	12 28	2 42		6 23				2 42
Murthly,	9 20	12 43	3 0						3 0
Stanley Junc	9 39	12 50	3 10		6 41				3 10
Arrive at									
Perth, ...	9 50	1 10	3 30		7 0				3 30
Arrive at									
Dundee, ...	11 20		5 18		8 20				
Edin. N.B.	1 5p	3 49	7 20		9 45				7 30
Do. E.&G.	1 0	4 25	6 40		9 55				
Glasgow,...	1 0	4 30	6 15		9 45				
	A.M.					A.M.			
Londn, G.N.	3 30	10 5			9 40				
		A.M.	A.M.						A.M.
Do. L.&N.W.		5 50	4 37		9 40				4 37

GREAT NORTH OF SCOTLAND RAILWAY.

TRAIN ARRANGEMENTS.

ON and after 1ST DECEMBER 1863, and until further notice, Trains will Arrive and Depart as under :—

Main Line.

DOWN TRAINS.

	& 3 1 & 3 A.M.	1 & 3 A.M.	Parl. Mail A.M.	1 & 3 1 & 3 P.M.	P.M	1 & 3 P.M.
London (via L. & N. W.) dep....	...	10·0	...	8·46	9.0	...
(via G. Northern), ...	...	10·0	...	...	9.15	...
Glasgow, per E. & G.),..	...	9·0p	...	6·40a	9·30a	...
Edinburgh, per S. C.,......	...	8·45	...	6·25	9·15	...
,, per N. B.,...	...	6·45	...	6·25	9 45	...
Perth, per S. N. E.,......	...	11·40	6·20	9·20	12·40p	...

	A.M.	A.M.	P.M.	P.M.	P.M.
Aberdeen,............dep. ...	8·0	11·0	1·20	4·40	6·45
Alford,................. ,,	...	7·40	10 45	...	4·20	...
Oldmeldrum,............ ,,	...	8·24	11·30	...	...	7·20
Banff & Macduff,.. ,,	...	6·59	10·0	12·40	...	6·5
Huntly,................. ,,	...	10·21	1·31	3·19	6·47	8·58
Banff (Har. Stn.),... ,,	...	9·15	12·20	...	5·0	...
Portsoy,................ ,,	...	9·27	12·25	...	5·14	...
Keith,................ arr. ...	10·51	2·5	3·57	7·20	9·30

	Parl. 1 & 3 A.M.	1 & 3 A.M.	1 & 3 P.M.	1 & 3 P.M.	1 & 3 P.M.
Keith,............dep.	7·30	11·0	...	4·5	7·40
Abernethy,............ ,,	6·30	10·20	...	3·0	...
Elgin, { arr.	9·5	12·40	...	5·42	9·30
{ dp.	9·10	1·0	3·10	6·15	...
Lossiemouth,........arr.	9·30	1·20	3·30	6·35	...

UP TRAINS.

	1 & 3 A.M.	Parl. 1 & 3 A.M.	1 & 3 P.M.	1 & 3 P.M.	1 & 3 1 & 3 P.M.
Lossiemouth,........dep. ...	...	9·50	2·0	3·45	7·16
Elgin, { arr.	...	...	10·10	2·20	4·5	7·30
{ dep.	7·40	...	11·15	...	4·15	7·55
Abernethy,............	6·30	...	10·20	...	3·0	...
Keith,............arr. ...	9·4	...	12·50	...	5 55	9·40

	1 & 3 A.M.	Mail. 1 & 3 A.M.	Parl. 1 & 3 A.M.	1 & 3 P.M.	1 & 3 P.M.	1 & 3 P.M.
Keith,............dep.	7·0	...	9·10	10·5	1·0	...	6·15
Portsoy,................	...	...	9·27	12·25	...	5·14
Banff (Har. Stn.),....	...	...	9·15	12·20	...	5·0
Huntly,................	7·33	9·41	10·45	1·31	...	6·47
Banff and Macduff,.....	6·50	...	10·0	12·40	...	6·5
Oldmeldrum,............	8 24	...	10·45	...	4·20	7·20
Alford,.................	7·40	...	10·45	...	3·45	6·20	9·0
Aberdeen,............arr.	9·45	11 55	1·5	...	3·45	6·20	9·0

	P.M.	P.M.	A.M.
Perth, per S. N. E. arr. ...	3·48	...	7·15	...	10·30
Edinburgh, per N. B. ...	7·20	...	9·52	...	1·0p
,, per S. C. ...	6·20	...	9·45	...	1·0
Glasgow, per E. & G. ...	6·15	...	9·45	...	1·0
London, via G. N....	...	...	9·40a	...	3·30a
,, via L. & N. W. ...	4·37a	...	9.40	...	...

Dufftown to join the Morayshire Railway on the north side of the Spey at Craigellachie and also up Speyside to Abernethy (later Nethy Bridge). The December 1863 timetable shows how the train service was basically an extension of the Dufftown service. Where connections were provided by the I&AJ line at Keith, journey times to Elgin were typically an hour longer via Craigellachie.

The year 1863 was a significant one in the development of railways in the north of Scotland. Not only was the Speyside line opened, but also the through route from Forres to Perth, thus realising the dream of a direct route south from Inverness. This had an immediate effect on the volume of traffic through Keith and the fortunes of the Great North. Travellers from Elgin and any points west of there for the south now avoided the route via Aberdeen, with its inconvenient break between the GNSR terminus at Waterloo and Guild Street, the station for the south trains. Even finding out train times between Aberdeen and Inverness became difficult. The I&AJ timetable was organised to show Keith at the end of a branch which connected with trains to Perth and the south at Forres.

Nor did the Dufftown line prosper as had been hoped. Traffic did rise slowly over the next few years, but so did working expenses. Although the extension to Craigellachie and the connection there to the Morayshire Railway provided a new route through to Elgin entirely under Great North control, passengers would not use it as trains took much longer than via the direct route and the I&AJ refused to exchange goods traffic at Elgin. It was to be the 1880s before this route was developed for through traffic. The Speyside line abjectly failed to live up to its expectations and brought little extra traffic to the Dufftown line. The construction of whisky distilleries did increase the traffic carried over the line, but this was a gradual process over the next half century.

Meanwhile, the Great North had been promoting various other branches in Aberdeenshire. Like the K&D, separate companies were floated to handle their construction, but all relied to a greater or lesser extent on GNSR support and all were worked by it. The Strathspey Railway in particular required so much capital from the GNSR that it was treated as an integral part of that company.

The K&D was in a similar position. Over half its capital cost had been covered by the GNSR, partly as borrowings. In 1864 and 1865, the revenue was not sufficient even to pay the bank and debenture interest, never mind a dividend to ordinary shareholders.

The capital account was complicated by the way the Balvenie extension was authorised and funded. As it was legally part of the Speyside Railway, it was included in the accounts of that company but was paid for by a subscription from the K&D. A dispute arose between the K&D directors appointed by the GNSR and the independent directors. The GNSR directors effectively ran the K&D, since they represented the bulk of the capital. Matters came to a head at the Ordinary Meeting held in November 1864, a protracted affair which had to be adjourned twice to obtain detailed financial information. The report in the *Banffshire Journal* occupied several pages of closely packed print. In the end, the local directors had to accept the Great North's view.

The financial impact on the GNSR of this rapid expansion was considerable. By 1865, it was clear that rationalisation was needed, so a Bill was promoted to enable the GNSR to absorb the K&D, the Strathspey and most of the other companies whose lines it operated. When this took effect in 1866, the consolidated accounts showed heavy indebtedness. In the same year a financial crisis linked to the over-hasty promotion of railway lines nationally led to a steep increase in interest rates. This left the company effectively bankrupt. It was only with the support of the banks in Aberdeen that a rescue was effected but several years of financial stringency followed. For the rest of the 1860s and through the 1870s, there was no more expansion.

The Highland Railway was formed in 1865 by the amalgamation of the I&AJ and the Inverness & Perth Junction. The Highland, too, was hit by the crisis of 1866 but managed to survive through the benefaction of its directors and major shareholders. It even managed to continue to pay a small dividend.

Traffic at Dufftown

From the Banffshire Journal, 3rd June 1862

The scene of bustle and activity presented at this station in the hitherto quiet and secluded valley of the Fiddich is something quite surprising. Every portion of the loading bank and every 'coign of vantage' that can be turned into a loading bank, has wagons alongside, and hands busily engaged unloading coals, manures, lime, stone and general merchandise. The whole of the traffic for Grantown passes through this station. There are two carriers – Shand with two carts and Bowie with four carts – each going twice a week between Dufftown Station and Grantown. Then there is the carrier M'Connachie, with two carts, going thrice a week between the station and Charlestown of Aberlour, making eighteen cart-loads weekly of general merchandise going into Strathspey. Beside this general and normal traffic, there is the conveyance of the materials for the contractors engaged in the construction of the Strathspey Line. All the rails for the Speyside and Morayshire Extension Railways have gone over the Dufftown Line. Then there is the carriage of the granite and freestone for the bridge across the Spey at Balnellan [Ballindalloch]. The granite is brought from Kemnay on the Alford Line; and the freestone comes by sea from Fifeshire to Aberdeen and thence is carried by rail to Dufftown. In the transport of these stones alone from Dufftown, it is calculated that a score of horses will be occupied till next August. Besides the carriers up Speyside, there are three carriers in the Glenlivat [sic] and Tomintoul traffic – Innes and Smith each with two carts twice a week; and Paul, with a cart weekly. There is also a carrier, Mackintosh, constantly employed carrying goods from the station to the store at Dufftown. The traffic for Glenlivat and Tomintoul will always be done at this station, even after the Strathspey line is opened, for the station at Balnellan is not greatly nearer Glenlivat, while to reach Balnellan there would of course be the additional mileage over the railway. The coal traffic is already very large – about 1300 tons having been received at the station since the opening. The coals are brought partly from Lossiemouth, but mostly from Aberdeen. There are as yet none from either Banff or Portsoy – which is surely a mistake on the part of the traders at these ports. A large business is being done in manures – and the Aberdeen Lime Company, the Northern Agricultural Company and the Macduff Commercial Company have each representatives and stores at the station. Messrs Kynoch, Keith, have also a store. All appear to do a large business. Mr Innes, Breaegach, has a grain store above the manure store of Messrs Kynoch. With all these combined, one may form some idea of the crowded state of the loading banks at the Dufftown Station, and will be prepared for the gratifying statement that on the morning of Tuesday last there were no fewer than 57 loaded wagons at the station. The train leaving at 5.25pm the previous Saturday comprised no fewer than 37 carriages. In fact the station is at present one of the most bustling on the whole of the Great North system, and we hear it stated that the receipts at this station alone would more than cover the whole working expenses of the entire Dufftown line.

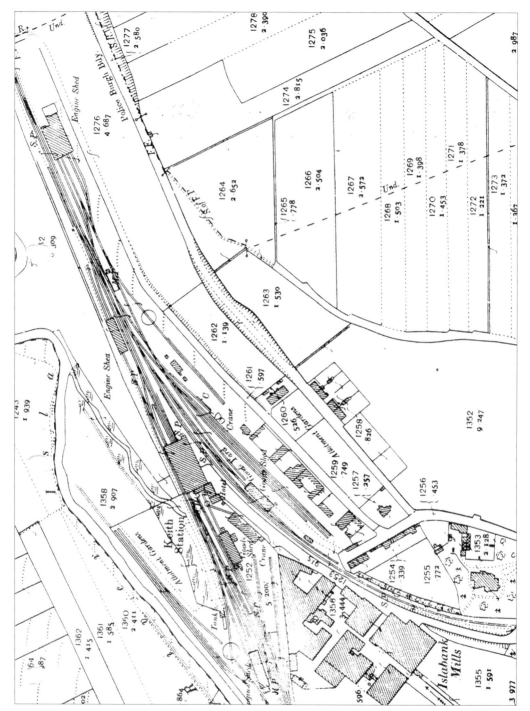

Second edition OS map of Keith, c1900. This shows the changes at the Highland end, where extensive goods sidings were added next to the engine shed and a goods depot built in the 'V' between the Elgin and Craigellachie lines, next to Kynoch's Islabank Mills. A new GNSR turntable has been provided but the doubling of its lines and resignalling have still to come.   (*Reproduced with permission of the Ordnance Survey.*)

Pre-Grouping Period

The facilities at Keith were gradually improved over the years. Refreshment rooms were an early addition; the GNSR Board resolved in October 1856 to erect first and third class rooms with a kitchen between them. The same meeting decided that an old store at Kittybrewster be moved to Keith for wagon repairs. Like the original goods shed, this must have been of wood. We know that the original goods shed was wooden as, on the night of 30th January 1859, the people of Keith were awakened by the sounds of the drum and the Kirk bell to discover part of the station in flames, though little more than the goods shed was actually destroyed. A covered goods wagon, an open wagon and a brake van inside were totally burnt out except for their iron work which was much damaged. Rebuilding of the shed is not recorded, although it is likely that the present stone structure dates from this time. Keith had, in fact, one of the few stone goods sheds on the Great North; nearly all were wooden.

In 1861, a new platform on the south side of the station was constructed for the Dufftown line. Since no early plans have survived, it is not known how much the layout of the sidings or the approach road changed, although it is possible that the approach road originally came in front of the houses opposite the main entrance to Kynoch's Mill; there was a level crossing here which latterly was available only to pedestrians.

The first edition OS map, surveyed 1868-1871, shows the present stone goods shed and separate Highland and GNSR engine sheds. The latter had four roads; the Minutes for April 1863 authorised expansion of the shed to tie in with the opening of the Speyside line. The map also shows a small shed on the north side of the line to the east of the platforms with separate

A Highland Small Ben, No. 5 Ben Vrackie *in front of the GNSR signal box, with a Highland 6-wheeler behind it. Presumably the train had arrived from Elgin and the coaches were being shunted into one of the other platforms ready to carry on to Aberdeen*   *(Highland Railway Society/Hunter collection)*

The Highland Railway end of Keith station looking west, with its goods shed to the left of the bay platform which was used by Buckie trains. The East signal box is perched above the goods shed and the West box can just be seen in the distance to the left of the loco shed. The turntable was to the right of the loco shed. Like many such stations in the north of Scotland, an old coach body has been put down as staff accommodation.
(Lens of Sutton collection)

sidings from the GNSR and Highland sides. The second edition map (c1900) shows this as an Engine shed, but it was in fact a carriage shed. This was mentioned in the Minutes of 1858 as it was included in the insurance cover, along with the passenger shed; in 1867 it was given a coat of pine varnish. It had disappeared by 1905.

The four-road Highland engine shed proved far too large so it was decided in 1868 to take down half the shed and re-erect it at Blair Atholl, where it still stands today.

The second edition map also marks as a hotel the building at the end of the bay platforms. This was a two storey structure which was later used as a telegraph office which was open 24 hours a day and was the switching centre for numerous telegraph circuits.

Gas for lighting was supplied by the Keith Gas Company but the Great North were not happy with the cost of gas so plans were prepared in 1862 for constructing a gas works at the station. A better offer from the Gas Company meant this was not necessary.

In 1864, the Company agreed to subscribe £40 towards a bridge over the River Isla at Keith. The road which passed to the south of the station crossed the line on a level crossing just east of the loco shed and then crossed the Isla to reach Newmill.

For several years after the amalgamation of 1866, the Great North was able to invest little in developing the railway. Gradually finances improved, debts were paid off and arrears of maintenance overcome. Traffic only increased slowly, with ups and downs caused, for instance, by animal disease. It was not until the 1880s and 1890s that significant changes occurred.

In 1877, the Highland decided to provide its own goods facilities at Keith and these were constructed in the land at the west end of the station, between the Highland platform and the Dufftown line. Several sidings and a goods shed were built. On the other side of the line, several more sidings were built for sorting through traffic which was now shuttled backwards and forwards to the Great North end. This must have added to both the time taken to forward goods and the cost involved. To help with the interchange of traffic which until then could only use the through platform line, the loop was connected to the Highland sidings at the west end.

By 1880, not only had the Great North recovered from its financial problems, but it had new management. William Ferguson of Kinmundy as Chairman and William Moffatt as the General Manager brought a new vigour to the running of the railway and sought to expand the system. An extension along the coast from Portsoy to Buckie and Portgordon had been authorised in 1863 but fell victim of the financial crisis of 1866. The fishing industry was expanding as larger, steam driven, boats were introduced. Ports had to be enlarged to match, one such being Buckie where a new harbour was opened in 1880 and this led to both the Highland and Great North promoting lines to plug this significant gap in railway facilities in the area. The Highland's solution was a branch from Keith over the sparsely populated hills to Buckie. Several changes were made to the west end of Keith to accommodate this service which started on 1st August 1884 with four mixed trains each way daily.

The Great North revived plans for an extension from Portsoy, but this time it continued the line all the way to Elgin. Not only would this tap the traffic of the coastal towns but it would provide a new route to Elgin and enable it to compete with the Highland more effectively. Work on the line took several years so it was not until 1886 that this route was finally completed. The Highland branch, which ran round the south side of Buckie, joined the GNSR line at Portessie, from where it was a short run to the Great North station by Buckie harbour.

The GNSR opened a connection at Grange to allow trains from the south to run directly to the Coast line; some trains split at Huntly and used this line while others continued to connect at Grange. When trains divided at Huntly, the second portion had to wait for the first one to clear the section to Rothiemay, so an exchange platform, called Cairnie Junction, was opened on 1st June 1898 at which trains could be split or joined.

The east end of Keith Junction from a Valentine's postcard. The Newmill road bridge is being built to replace the level crossing. Just to its left can be seen Newmill box, which was the end of the double track from Aberdeen until the station area was resignalled in 1905.

The Great North also wanted to increase its revenue from traffic to the Highland by developing the Dufftown line as a through route to Elgin. Until the 1880s, trains from Aberdeen normally connected with Highland trains at Keith and also with stopping trains to Elgin via Dufftown which reached Elgin well after the Highland ones had done. Moreover, the arrangements for routing through tickets did not allow the Great North to collect any extra revenue if the passenger used the Dufftown line. Through tickets were nipped with a number allocated by the Railway Clearing House to show the route they had been used on; at the end of each journey the tickets were collected and sent to the Clearing House which divided up the revenue to each company over which the passenger had travelled. All this of course was done manually. A number was finally allocated to the route via Dufftown between 1880 and 1884.

In the summer of 1885, as a consequence of the speeding up of mail services from London to Scotland, the Highland, with little notice, retimed one of their trains from Keith so that it left too early to connect with the main morning train from Aberdeen. The Great North went to court to stop them doing this but also introduced the first through express to Elgin via Dufftown. The legal challenges lasted on and off for another 11 years. The Great North wanted through carriages and freight exchanged at Elgin, especially after the Coast route opened in 1886. As part of the postal improvements, a Post Office Sorting Carriage was introduced between Aberdeen and Elgin and this operated over the Dufftown line initially; it was transferred to the Coast route when that opened. Only at busy times, such as Christmas, did one operate via Dufftown.

When the dispute with the Highland was settled in 1897, a much more generous through service was offered, with about half the trains running fast via Dufftown. This soon proved to be over generous, but the route continued to carry its share of that traffic.

In 1886, the Great North agreed to the erection of a siding at Mill o'Wood, about 2 miles

This postcard entitled "Crachie, Dufftown" shows the siding from Parkmore running down the valley and crossing the Huntly road on a level crossing. Mortlach distillery is off the left hand side of the photograph. The line was built without parliamentary powers so the legality of the level crossing was challenged by the Dufftown Burgh Police Commissioners. Trains shunting at Mortlach could cause considerable delays to traffic over the crossing.

east of Keith, for a Lime Works owned by James Kemp. The link to the quarry about a mile from the main line can still be traced. The earthworks, cuttings and bridge abutments extant could not have carried anything more than about 2 foot gauge. They lead down to the top of the kilns, via a hefty embankment made from waste material. Then from the bottom of the kilns the route (still only about 2 foot gauge) goes on downhill, crosses a stream and a field, runs across the road on the level, skirts round a shoulder of a hill on the level and comes out against the main line. Here the current day railway boundary fence comes away from the track, to go round the site of the siding. At the railway end is the ruin of a house, shown as "Mill of Wood Gatehouse"

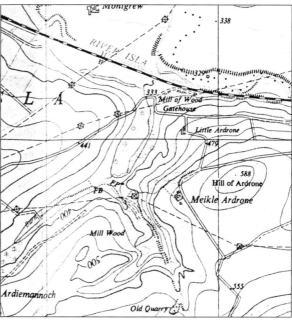

1957 OS Map of Mill o'Wood siding

on the 1957 map which also shows some of the earthworks near the quarry. The scale of the railway works is impressive for such a relatively small quarry.

Several improvements were made on the line to Dufftown during the 1890s, such as the sidings to Glendullan and Mortlach distilleries and the new station buildings at Drummuir and Keith Town. These are described on page 40.

The increased train services do not seem to have led to any enhancement of the passenger facilities at Keith. Complaints made in 1907 pointed out that the buildings had been little altered since their erection in 1856. This seems to have triggered action, as the Board proposed on 5th March 1907 to convert the first class refreshment room into a new entrance hall and provide a new refreshment room on the ground floor of the former hotel, if the works could be done at reasonable cost. The Company must have been conscious that, by then, Keith was one of the few major stations which had not been rebuilt; Elgin, Fraserburgh, Inverurie, Banchory and Aboyne all had new station buildings and the rebuilding of Aberdeen Joint was about to start. Maybe the cost of this inhibited work elsewhere.

To handle increasing traffic on the main line, double track was gradually installed from the Aberdeen end, finally reaching Newmill, just south of Keith in 1898. Here the level crossing was replaced by an overbridge. The GNSR turntable was originally between the engine shed and goods yard; as part of the improvements, a 50 foot turntable and new water tower were provided at an isolated position east of the Newmill Road bridge.

The First World War placed a great strain on the Highland, so all through trains between Aberdeen and Inverness were operated by the Great North until 1917, when services were severely curtailed. The Buckie branch was an early casualty, closing completely on 9th August 1915 as a 'temporary' measure. The track was removed for use elsewhere. After the war it was relaid and preparations made to reopen the line in 1926, by which time local bus services had started so the LMS decided not to reopen after all. Only the short section to Aultmore was used, to serve the distillery there.

The Junction station from the east end in LNER days, after removal of the roof. D42 No.6810 heads a rake of Great North six wheelers on a train which could have either been a Coast line or main line stopping service. As usual, plenty of van space was provided for luggage and parcels. The tall signal above the carriages applied to trains coming on the Highland route from Elgin, its height enabling it to be seen from beyond the Highland locomotive shed. *(GNSRA collection)*

Pre-grouping locomotives were the norm at Keith throughout the 1930s. Here two Small Bens, Ben Armin *and* Ben Hope, *make a spirited getaway towards Elgin with one cattle wagon and two coaches. Double heading, such as in this instance, was often necessary to balance locomotive duties.* *(J L Stevenson collection)*

After 1923

The Great North and Highland Railways lost their independence in 1923 when they became part of the London & North Eastern and London, Midland & Scottish Railways respectively. Management gradually became more centralised. Local staff were left to carry on much as they had always done but with growing road competition, initiatives to develop new traffic were few and investment money scarce.

In the late 1920s, the condition of the overall roof at the station must have been deteriorating as it was completely removed. Awnings were provided over the bay and Highland platforms, supported on metal beams. The Refreshment room survived until early British Railways days.

The period 1920 to 1950 saw little change to the track and signalling at Keith. Some upper quadrant signal arms were installed in a piecemeal fashion. Since the train service altered little, there was no need to make other changes, although bus competition led to a gradual decline in patronage, especially for shorter distance journeys.

The Great North had started regular excursion trains from Aberdeen to the Speyside line in June 1905, running on summer Wednesdays (Aberdeen half day closing) and Saturday. These were continued in the 1920s and by the late 1930s were included in the timetable as ordinary trains. A through excursion from Aberdeen to Inverness, running on summer Thursdays and complete with restaurant car, was introduced in the mid-1930s. A report in a contemporary magazine showed that it stopped at the east end short of the platform and engines were changed there. It was often double-headed.

The Second World War saw many people return to the railways but traffic levels quickly resumed their downward trend by the time British Railways took charge in 1948. During the

Keith GNSR Shed in LNER days, with a nice line-up of Great North 4-4-0s and an ex-Great Eastern B12. The tight clearance between locos and door frames is obvious. The photograph was taken during a group visit; some of the party are in front of the right hand locomotive.   *(Photo : Keith & District Heritage Group)*

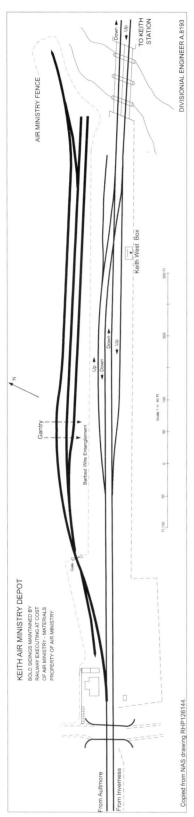

War the Air Ministry built a gas factory west of Keith to produce hydrogen for barrage balloons and other gases, shown in the map on the left. This was served by a new siding which made a trailing connection to the Aultmore line. The heavy traffic, mainly gas cylinders, was worked within the factory by its own Ruston 48hp Diesel shunter. The factory closed in 1955 and the site is now occupied by bonded warehouses.

In 1948, control of all the railways in Scotland was unified on the formation of the Scottish Region of British Railways. This did not bring any immediate change in the operation of the lines to Keith. Some through locomotive working between Aberdeen and Inverness was introduced but, in the main, Keith retained its operational importance. The coal crisis of 1951 saw the withdrawal of some passenger trains, initially on a temporary basis but they never resumed. The drift away from the railways, both in passenger and freight traffic continued.

In the early 1950s an *Aberdeen Evening Express* reporter travelled to Inverness via Dufftown, and commented that intermediate stations had seen better days and that traffic between Keith and Elgin was sparse. He wrote: "There was something rather pathetic in the way the gold braided Station Masters walked the length of their platforms, shouting station names".

With larger locomotives in use in the 1950s, the narrow arched doors to the engine shed became a hazard and were removed. A steel beam was installed over the openings which now spanned two tracks each.

The British Railways Modernisation Plan of 1955 was meant to stem mounting losses by introducing diesel traction and funding many other improvements. Steam was eliminated from the area in 1961, except on the Banff branch for which Keith provided the locomotives. The number of employees at Keith was reduced. The previous year, diesel multiple units operating on a 2½ hour schedule were introduced between Aberdeen and Inverness and were an immediate success. The service was expanded to four trains each way the following year and other services re-arranged around them, further reducing the need for staff and locomotives based at Keith.

Despite the investment, losses on the railways as a whole continued to mount. Dr Beeching was appointed chairman of the British Transport Commission in 1961 with a mandate to reduce those losses. His *Reshaping of British Railways*, published in 1963, forecast the end of all services north

The Gas Factory at the west end of Keith as seen from the Tarmore Bridge over the Highland line. Keith West box can be seen in the distance. the corrugated iron shed behind the chimney pots in the immediate foreground housed the Ruston loco which shunted the sidings. (Keith & District Heritage Group)

of Aberdeen except the through trains to Inverness serving principal stations only. All local goods depots would also close. Whatever the rights and wrongs of Dr Beeching's plan, many trains on rural lines such as those in the Keith area were used by very few passengers; it was hard to justify running nearly empty trains. The proposals took several years to implement in the north east. The Banff branch shut on 6th July 1964, whereupon the remaining steam locos at Keith disappeared, followed later that year, on 7th December, by the poorly patronised local stations on the Highland line to Elgin. The Speyside line lost its passenger services the following year on 18th October and the goods service on the stub of the Buckie line serving the distillery at Aultmore stopped on 3rd October 1966.

It was more difficult to organise replacement bus services for the Coast and Dufftown lines and the local stations on the main line south of Keith but eventually their last trains ran on Saturday 4th May 1968.

Goods services had a slower run-down. Many of the smaller goods stations closed in 1964 but freight services through to Aviemore remained after the passenger trains ceased. These were cut

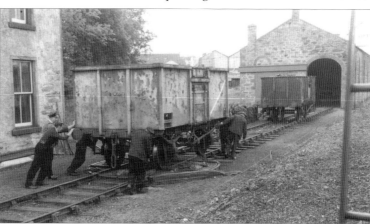

Although a shunting loco was employed at Keith, it could not reach the end of the Highland's goods shed siding. A horse might at one time have been employed or it might have been dragged by a rope attached to a loco on the next track, but that practice had to stop as it was too dangerous. Here manpower came to the rescue.
(Welsh Railway Circle, Stratton Collection)

The station viewed from near the signal box in 1966. An Aberdeen bound train is coming out of the Highland platform. The sidings on the left are still quite busy. Unusually, the signals here are on the right of the tracks to which they refer; the left hand signal is for the goods loop on the left and the right hand one for the down line in the centre. The Dufftown line platform is on the left. (Norris Forrest/GNSRA)

Strong winds affected the area on Saturday 31st January 1953. The 7.10a.m. train from Keith to Elgin, headed by B1 No.61242 Sir Alexander Reith Gray, got held up as it approached Drummuir. It had to stop after leaving Auchindachy to disentangle the engine from a wagon sheet and then a little further on was halted by a tree across the line. There were only three passengers in the train – all railwaymen. Trees continued to fall and eventually there were no less than eleven trees on the engine and the tender alone, and many more on the coaches. It was late on Saturday night before the whole train got free. (Ross Kerby collection)

back in 1968 to Aberlour and then Dufftown in 1971, where coal traffic continued until 16th May 1983. The section from Craigellachie to Elgin remained open for freight until November 1968.

On a positive note, a grain depot was established at Dufftown for bulk transport. A large silo was erected in 1966, followed by a second one the year after, served by new sidings. For a while, block trains ran from Doncaster bringing a variety of motive power to the line, including Class 40s. The grain traffic also disappeared in the early 1980s, although the line remained available for grain and coal traffic until the end of 1984. After years of disuse, the unsightly silos were removed in 2005.

Keith Junction remained open for goods traffic during the 1970s and 1980s, but British Railways continued the process of rationalisation and only accepted traffic which was profitable. The loco shed became disused after 1968 and the building and surrounding land were later sold off to Chivas Regal, who built a new bond on the site which incorporated the north wall of the loco shed. Some whisky in bulk tank wagons was handled for a time to Dalmuir, near Glasgow, but even that proved to be uneconomic and was transferred to road haulage. In the late 1990s and early 2000s, timber traffic was handled for shipment to pulp mills but the cyclic nature of timber cutting has meant that local sources had dried up by 2006. The sidings at Keith remain, nominally available for traffic, but may need attention if they are to be used again.

By a stroke of luck, the fortunes of the Dufftown line rose again after goods traffic ceased. Local enterprise, in the form of Grampian Railtours, started operating regular excursions under the title *Northern Belle* from Aberdeen in 1984. Stock from the overnight London service, which would otherwise have lain unused at Aberdeen, was utilised for a good day out to visit one of the distilleries at Dufftown. The line also became popular with charter trains from the south. When sectorisation was introduced by British Railways, the Dufftown line was in the odd position of being allocated to Inter City. Rising costs and the need to spend money on maintenance eventually brought an end to the use of the line by excursion trains and it was taken out of use on 1st April 1991 after about 300 *Northern Belles* had operated.

A short section at the Keith end was retained as part of the national network so that specials, mainly the *Royal Scotsman* luxury tourist train, could operate to Strathisla Distillery, where a platform constructed of scaffolding and timber enabled passengers to alight from one coach. After it closed the track was lifted between the end of the Junction station platform and Keith Town station. At the latter, the wooden buildings were demolished in the 1980s. Keith is still

In later years, the buildings at Keith exhibited a run-down appearance. This is the view from the approach road, with the Dufftown platform on the right.
(Jonathon Dransart/GNSRA)

Drummuir station staff pose for a photograph which, judging by the uniforms, is likely to have been taken between 1920 and 1923. From the left, Jas. Asher, Clerk; Eddie Angus, possibly porter/signalman, James Ogg, Agent who was at Drummuir from 1915 to 1929.

(Mike Stephen colln)

visited by the *Royal Scotsman* where it parks in the Dufftown line platform. Other special trains visit occasionally.

To the east, major alterations took place on the main line in the late 1960s to reduce operating costs and enable trains to operate at higher speeds. The double track from Aberdeen to Keith was reduced to single, apart from the section between Insch and Kennethmont, and a passing place provided at the east end of Keith station. Tokenless block working was introduced from Aberdeen to Elgin, thus avoiding the physical exchange of tokens with all the dangers that that entailed. The track to the through platform was realigned for faster approach, finally achieving the objective propounded by Major Marindin in 1884. The Dufftown platform has been retained for use by passenger trains terminating at Keith to avoid entering the single line section to Elgin.

When the track was removed from the two bay platforms the area was left empty. By 1983, the gap had been filled in and a few plant-pots installed to improve its appearance. The buildings remained, with plenty of empty space. Something new was clearly necessary so in 1987, all the buildings were demolished and the present light and airy structure erected close to the through platform. Only that part of the overall roof which protected this platform was retained. A new car park was provided with turning facilities for connecting buses. The new

---

"I was a trainee clerk at Drummuir at the end of 1943. Mr Clark, the station master, was rather a strict individual whose hobby was bee keeping. He would not allow me to do any book keeping until I was reasonably proficient in operating the telegraph instrument, which at that time was virtually the sole means of communication between stations on the GNSR section of the LNER. My other duties were daily pumping of water to a storage tank which fed the station toilets and assisting in chaining long round timber on to bogie bolster wagons. Traffic dealt with at that time consisted of timber at Loch Park siding and Drummuir, oatmeal at Auchindachy, whisky, coal and empty barrels, etc., at Towiemore. I cycled to my home in Dufftown and had my dinner at the home of Charlie Ogston, one of the signalmen; Charlie's father was the permanent way inspector at Craigellachie for many years."

Ian Ritchie, 1993

In the 1950s, William Low operated the bus service between Dufftown and Tomintoul. The vehicle was a Leyland PS1-1, registration EVD580.
(Graham Maxtone colln)

building, on the site of the former bay platforms, was occupied on Sunday 31st July 1988 and officially opened by the Convener of Grampian Region Council, Geoff Hadley, on 19th August. The whole project cost £200,000, of which the Regional Council contributed £20,000 towards the car park and BR regional parcels operation £23,000 since there was still a considerable parcels traffic. Presumably because of increased maintenance costs, the roof over the platform and protective screen on the north side were removed in 1998 and a new porch erected on the platform side. The rebuilt station did not provide accommodation for local signalling and other maintenance staff who are accommodated in a row of Portacabins at the east end of the platform.

Train operation passed from British Rail to the National Express Group in 1997, although the previous "ScotRail" brand name was retained. In 2004, the Aberdeen-based First Group took over. Bus connections are provided to several trains to enable passengers to reach some of the towns off the railway.

Keith as rebuilt in 1989. The part of the old roof which was retained to provide shelter for passengers boarding trains was later removed. *(Photo Keith Fenwick)*

Although Strathisla Distillery never had a rail connection, a short platform was built for the use of passengers on the Royal Scotsman. It was in use by 1988 but was closed in August 1993 on safety grounds. It was provided with genuine GNSR oil lamps. The footbridge behind carried a path to the Distillery over the railway and was one of the few lattice bridges on the Great North. (Keith Fenwick)

Keith Town was always much more convenient than the Junction station for local passengers, so much so that there were trains which did not stop at the Junction and called at Town instead. Some workings started or terminated there. This is the 5.18pm from Keith Town to Cairnie Junction in July 1959. It would have been propelled empty from the Junction station. At Cairnie, a connection was made to a train from Aberdeen to Elgin. Until 1959, the train had run from Grange direct to Grange North Junction and continued to Elgin, with a connection at Grange with the train from Aberdeen. (Douglas Hume)

Along the Line to Dufftown

Finding a route out of Keith for the Dufftown line was not easy. For the first mile, it closely followed the river, passing the Castle and then Strathisla distillery. No siding was installed here, but when the Royal Scotsman started to include the distillery on its itinerary a short platform was constructed of scaffolding and wood.

The line then reached Keith Town station, known as Earlsmill until 1st May 1897, where originally a small stone building was constructed. This was replaced by a wooden one about the time of renaming. While this was basically to a standard contemporary design, it was located in a cutting so a second building was built on the access road at the top of the cutting and internal stairs built to connect the two. The original buildings disappeared during the 1980s, so the KDRA have constructed a replica of the wooden two-part building. Some changes were made to meet modern building standards.

Beyond the station, the railway passes under the main road from Aberdeen to Inverness and then runs past Strathmill distillery, which was served by a siding with a trailing connection for trains going towards Dufftown. This siding was open by 1877 and was out of use at least twice before closure on 3rd October 1966. It was reopened in 1978 for deliveries of grain. Fortunately the siding remains and is used by the KDRA for locomotive hauled and works trains. The points are hand operated.

Following the general south-westerly direction of the route to Dufftown, the line now strikes across open country to Auchindachy, 3¼ miles from Keith, where the station consisted of a single platform with stone building and sidings. It was called Botriphinie when opened, but was renamed on 1st June 1863. A second platform and passing loop was added in 1892.

The upper building at Keith Town, photographed in 1973, provided a covered entrance to the steps down to the main building at platform level. This has been recreated by the K&DR, but set back from the road and with a central entrance to the lower building. *(Keith Fenwick)*

Stathmill Distillery just beyond Keith Town station was served by a siding which still exists. It had not been used for some time when this photograph was taken in May 1989 but was used at least once after then, in September that year, when it received several Polybulk wagons. Because of the length of the siding, these had to be delivered two at a time. Short sidings such as this were not designed for bulk deliveries in bogie wagons.   *(Keith Fenwick)*

Auchindachy looking towards Keith in the 1950s. Although there are several wagons in the sidings, they were likely to be in store. It was quite common to park stored wagons in out of the way places at that time. Originally there would have been a wooden footbridge, but by the 1930s these were rotting, so the LNER replaced them throughout the Great North area with ones made from old rails.   *(J L Stevenson)*

Towiemore distillery from a postcard dated around 1936. The Dufftown line is in the foreground. The section nearest the camera, behind the telegraph pole, remains in use as offices. (Ron Smith colln)

Originally all trains called here but by the early 1950s only a token one or two trains each way called daily. Goods services were withdrawn on 20th April 1964 and the loop closed on 1st September of that year. Staff had been withdrawn by then and so the station building sank into decay until rescued in the 1990s and for use as the basis of an attractive house.

After another 1½ miles, Towiemore is reached. This has a complicated history. A siding was first brought into use on 1st June 1863 known as Drummuir Lime Kilns. It later became known as Botriphnie (not to be confused with Auchindachy which was also originally known by the same name), certainly by December 1884. The siding received coal to fire the kilns and despatched bags of crushed quicklime or slaked lime. There was a quarry about half a mile north of the station; later the quarry built a 2ft gauge line to the station. Traffic from the quarry

Towiemore from a down train in 1953. The body of third class 5-compartment third No.127, dating from 1865, had been installed at the station in 1924 and survived as station offices until closure. The building nearest to the camera was later added to provide storage and, roofless, can still be seen.

(J A N Emslie)

ceased by the early 1960s. A distillery was opened at Towiemore in the 1890s, directly served from a new siding. The distillery ceased to distil whisky in 1936 and was then used as a maltings and for storage, with a break during the War when it was used by army regiments as a base for mountain and winter training. It ceased to be used by the distilling industry in 1993 and some of the buildings were then demolished. The remaining building and a new structure are now used by LH Stainless, an engineering company involved in process engineering, vessel manufacture and design services for the distilling, brewing and offshore industries. In 1888 a small signal box was installed on the opposite side of the line from the siding. This was replaced by a ground frame in 1896 but the structure continued in use as an office for the Agent and was extant in the 1960s. A passenger platform was finally erected in 1924 and an old coach body installed on it to act as booking office and waiting room. It was not until 1937 that the station was advertised in the timetables. The station retained a good passenger service until the line closed in 1968 but goods services ceased on 2nd November 1964.

A further 1½ miles brings the line to Drummuir, about half a mile from the village. The first edition OS map shows a single platform, small building, two sidings and goods shed. With the introduction of fully interlocked signalling and to accommodate growing traffic, the Board agreed in 1892 to spend £2,480 at Drummuir. A loop was installed here in 1894 and a new station building provided in contemporary wooden style at an estimated cost of £348. On the new platform, a small verandah was provided as shelter at a cost of £36.

One of the most attractive stretches of the line follows as it skirts Loch Park. This shallow water was used for bonspiels and so in December 1894 the Board agreed to provide a platform at the north end of the loch. Drummuir Curlers Platform appears to have been used for several years.

The line now descends through a cutting towards Dufftown. Just before the Fiddich Viaduct already described, a siding was provided on 5th October 1891 to serve Parkbeg Quarry but it was subsequently known as Parkmore Limeworks Siding. In 1900, a line was built from this

Drummuir from the Keith end in 1964. The sidings had been cleared of wagons and the station looks little used. By 1968 the loop had gone, together with the up platform.   *(Norris Forrest/GNSRA)*

The siding at Parkmore left the main line to the east of the Fiddich viaduct, just behind the wagons in the distance. The signal in the centre is the down distant for Dufftown. The track on the left in the foreground led to Glendullan and Mortlach. This view dates from March 1966.

(Norris Forrest/ GNSRA)

siding down to Mortlach Distillery and a neighbouring woollen mill there, serving Glendullan Distillery on the way. Just before Mortlach, the line crossed the road on a level crossing. The line was built on private land without parliamentary authority, but Crachie crossing over the public road was another matter. The Dufftown Police Commissioners did not give their consent but the Great North went ahead and laid the rails. Court action ensued but was eventually settled.

Shunting at Mortlach involved using the level crossing and this could cause congestion. One woman recalled that when she was a girl her route to school involved cycling over the crossing.

This view of Dufftown was taken in September 1967, when the first grain silo was under construction. The station is off to the right in the distance, with the sidings to the right of centre. The points in the foreground gave access to the goods yard.   *(Norris Forrest/GNSRA)*

Dufftown seen from the rear of a Keith bound train in October 1954. The local bus provides a connection to the train. Wooden stays to support the goods shed suggest that it was in danger of collapse; many similar Great North goods sheds decayed in a similar way.   *(J L Stevenson)*

Sometimes she was held up by the loco being on the crossing for quite a while, making her late for school. One morning, there it was again and after waiting for a while she screwed up her courage to ask the driver, who was leaning out of his cab, how long he was going to be, as if she was late to school again she was going to get a row, or worse. The driver got down off the loco, lifted her and then her bike over the crossing gates, escorted her around the loco, and lifted her and the bike back onto the road again, so she got to school on time that day!

The branch was worked from the Dufftown end. The train would be locked into the siding at Parkmore and then the staff for the section from Dufftown to Drummuir returned by foot to Dufftown. When the train completed its shunting, the reverse process let it back on to the main line. The section to Mortlach was closed on 23rd March 1964 and the remaining part to Glendullan and Parkmore on 7th November 1966.

Dufftown station is situated about half a mile north of the village on the road to Craigellachie. It was provided with a passing loop, several sidings and a goods shed. The first edition OS map also shows a wagon turntable which was used to deliver coal wagons into Glenfiddich Distillery. Considerable traffic was carried on at this station as it served not only the town but also the adjacent glens up to Tomintoul. However its distance from the town gave competing road services an advantage when they were developed in the twentieth century. Apart from new signalling and some additional sidings, little changed. The original stone building still stands. In the mid-1960s, the station was chosen as the site for grain storage silos. Grain was brought up from the south in regular trains and then shipped on by road to the various distilleries. This traffic lasted until the late 1970s, as already described.

Beyond Dufftown, the line turned northwards to Craigellachie, running alongside the River Fiddich. This section was retained after the line closed to passengers in 1968 to serve the coal depot at Aberlour until that closed on 15th November 1971. Some years later it was converted into a footpath as a spur of the Speyside Way, although part of the trackbed above the river has collapsed and needs to be treated with caution. It connects today with the Isla Way to Keith.

Locomotives and Rolling Stock

The locomotives and carriages used reflected the importance the two companies placed on the train services to Keith; the Great North employed its best engines while engines cascaded from its main line were used by the Highland. The Great North, of course, relied on 4-4-0s for most of its trains and produced a succession of elegant designs. Earlier ones had outside cylinders and very little protection for the crew. James Manson, the locomotive engineer in the 1880s, changed to inside cylinders and provided a rudimentary cab but it was not until the late 1890s that proper cabs became the norm. Apart from superheating, locomotive design advanced little in the remaining GNSR years.

Highland engines were also nearly all 4-4-0s, its larger locos being needed on the Perth line. The Small and Large Bens frequently appeared and, after 1906, worked through to Aberdeen on some services. 4-4-0 tanks were used on the Buckie branch, initially Jones Tank No.59 *Highlander* and later Yankee Tank No.14 *Portessie*. The Highland had a nice habit of naming engines after the lines they worked.

After the Grouping, the LNER could not afford new engines for the GNSR section, but did transfer ex-Great Eastern 4-6-0s of class B12 in the late 1920s to cope with increasing loads. Ex-Highland Castle class 4-6-0s appeared at the west end of the station.

By the 1950s, much more modern motive power became available, although some of the GNSR 4-4-0s lingered on working lighter trains, especially on the Speyside line. Several LNER designed class B1 4-6-0s were allocated when new and worked many of the passenger trains. The GNSR shed at Keith, which was second in importance to Kittybrewster and had a larger allocation

Most GNSR locomotives were 4-4-0s and these lasted well into the 1950s as a reminder of just how attractive locomotives could be. Class D40 No.62273 George Davidson *was still regularly used on services such as Speyside.*
(Photo Eric Greig)

The ex-Great Eastern B12s were the best locos on the line from the early 1930s to the late 1940s. No.61508 is shunting at Keith. (Graham Maxtone colln)

than Elgin, took on additional work when the Highland's shed was closed in early BR days. As a result, ex-LMS types were now shedded there and could be found working on GNSR metals. These included several Caledonian engines, among them 0-4-4Ts for the Banff branch, a few Midland-designed class 2 4-4-0s and, of course, the ubiquitous Black 5s which had revolutionised train working on the Highland main line in the 1930s and went on to operate nearly all the ex-Highland lines by the mid-1950s. Some other LNER types, such as the ex-Great Northern K2 2-6-0s and ex-North British 4-4-0s and 0-6-0s, also appeared. BR introduced a range of standard designs in the 1950s. Those allocated to the north east were mixed traffic types for light or medium duties, Class 2 2-6-0s, Class 4MT 2-6-0s and Class 4MT 2-6-4Ts. When Keith shed closed to steam in June 1961, it had an allocation of 23 locomotives.

British Railways had little to do with diesel motive power in the early 1950s but made a sudden change with the Modernisation Plan of 1955. Lines north of Perth and Aberdeen were easy to convert to diesel traction and this took place in 1960 and 1961. With the exception

Keith shed was a fascinating place in the 1950s. By the time this photo was taken on 15th August 1959, the older engines had gone but there was still a Caley 0-6-0, an LMS 2P, 40617, and a couple of BR standards, 80114 and 78052. The rebuilt entrance to the shed is clearly visible.   (Photo Douglas Hume)

The modernisation plan resulted in the construction of a variety of diesel designs from different builders but with varying degrees of success. The North British Type 2s, despite their attractive design, were never reliable but 20 were allocated to the Great North lines. One of the class waits at Keith to take a single coach, most likely as a connection to Cairnie Jct. (Ray Nolton)

of the Class 2s retained to work the Banff branch with its mixed trains, steam disappeared from Keith in June 1961. Diesel motive power was as much a mixture as the steam power it replaced. Four wheeled railbuses, uncomfortable for a short journey but a test of stamina for the Aviemore to Keith run, were used on the Speyside line. Two car Craven multiple units and North British Type 2 locos took over passenger workings while some English Electric Type 1s, later class 20, were provided for goods workings plus Barclay 204 h.p. locos for shunting at Keith. The North British Type 2s were notoriously unreliable and disappeared by 1967, to be replaced by the much more successful Sulzer engined Type 2s, such as those which later became classes 24, 26 and 27.

The through Aberdeen to Inverness trains introduced in 1960 were operated by 3-car Swindon built multiple units which included a small buffet. These were the mainstay after the closures of 1968. In turn they gave way to locomotive haulage in the late 1970s, with Type 2s of classes 26 or 27 initially and then class 47s, until the arrival of Class 156 diesel units in the late 1980s. Locomotive haulage using class 37s then reappeared for a time before Class 158s took over and these operate a good proportion of trains today, with others worked by Class 170s which provide the services south of Aberdeen and on the Inverness main line.

Coaching stock in the early days was exclusively 4-wheeled. Admired at the time for their smooth riding, they were in turn replaced by 6-wheelers and then bogie coaches. Even so, many of the local services were still worked by rattling 6-wheelers in the 1930s. The Great North built some very comfortable bogie coaches for through working to Inverness but the LNER and LMS allocated very little new stock to the services. In the 1950s, in an effort at standardisation, ex-LMS vehicles were drafted in to work all the main services through Keith. BR Mark 1s made their appearance towards the end of the 1950s, operating on most of the loco-hauled services by 1968. At the end of locomotive haulage, BR Mark 2 stock was used.

Keith Junction signal box, built 1905, was a typical late GNSR box of wooden construction. Some of the panelling details are similar to contemporary wooden station buildings. Since this photo was taken in 1970, internal refurbishment has taken place to give the signallers more suitable working conditions but the exterior has not been altered.   (George L Pring/Railway Record of the British Isles)

The other signal boxes on the line to Dufftown were installed eariler than Keith and were to a plainer design. This is the main box at Dufftown, the largest on the line. The other box there was at the north end of the down platform.   (George L Pring/Railway Record of the British Isles)

Signalling and Track Layout

Signalling requirements when the lines were opened were rudimentary. Each station had to be equipped with a signal to admit trains to the station, often referred to as the distance or distant signal, and one to authorise them to leave. Points were locally controlled, but there was no interlocking with signals. The stationmaster had overall control and directed men to operate the points and signals.

All the lines to Keith were single and this presented added dangers. The Great North was ahead of many southern companies in installing the telegraph and the I&AJ followed suit. Messages were sent and acknowledged between stations before a train was sent on its way. Both companies were early believers in the block system where only one train was allowed on each single line section at a time. By 1862, the telegraph was being used by the Great North to enforce this. Of course, this still relied on the staff following the rules; in 1867, the Agent at Keith was fined £2 for sending a train to Grange without previously giving a signal on the electric telegraph, per the Company's rules. A circular was then sent out to all servants that any failure to signal using the telegraph, or anyone not reporting such an incident, would lead to dismissal.

Both the Highland and Great North took a long time to improve the safety of their signalling, arguing that their method of working suited the traffic and had not caused any accidents. However, by the 1880s pressure was increasing. The Board of Trade had power to insist on interlocked points and signals for new lines and so when the Highland's Buckie branch was opened on 1st August 1884 a signal box with 21 levers and a passing loop was provided at the new junction. The Board of Trade Inspector, Major Marindin, added to his report that the signal arrangements at Keith were unsatisfactory; the Highland was willing to interlock the west end of the station if the Great North allowed them to do so. However, he stated that the proper way of improving the station was to continue the centre lines through the existing buildings forward as a double line as far as the junction with the Buckie branch.

In 1889, the BoT obtained power to require interlocking on all existing lines, although time was allowed for implementation. A second Highland signal box was provided in 1889, an elevated structure next to the goods shed. It was to be several years before the GNSR side was properly controlled; the company concentrated at first on intermediate stations, possibly arguing that trains travelled much more slowly at places such as Keith than they did at wayside stations.

Work was also in hand to double the track on the

The points at the end of the Dufftown line were too far from the signal cabin to be worked directly so a ground frame, known as Keith North, was provided on the platform to work them and Kynoch's Gates, the level crossing just beyond, under supervision of the main cabin. This was usually the job of a porter at the station. (Ian Scrimgeour)

line from the south, so this delayed improvements at Keith even further. Doubling reached Insch in 1888 and Huntly in 1896. A new viaduct at Rothiemay had to be built so a temporary block post was established at Avochie to the south of the bridge to enable the double track from Huntly to be opened on 19th January 1898. Two days earlier, the section from Rothiemay to Newmill, just south of Keith, became double. Then on 30th April 1900 the new bridge at Rothiemay was opened and double track was available throughout to a point where the Newmill road crossed the railway on the level. A signal cabin was provided there while the overbridge was built. Single line continued into Keith station where a cabin referred to as Keith Ground Signal Cabin, had opened on 3rd February 1898 at the south end of the platform, but it is clear from subsequent remarks that this did not provide full interlocking.

Another uncertainty was the plan to double the GNSR line westward. In 1895, it had been decided to seek parliamentary powers for doubling the line from Keith to Elgin with deviations and other improvements recommended by the Engineer, but it was not until 1898 that these powers were obtained and then only the sections from Keith Junction to a point near Dufftown and between Longmorn and Elgin were authorised. No steps seem to have been taken to put this work into effect and the powers lapsed in 1901.

So, despite a letter from the Board of Trade in March 1900 complaining about the uncompleted interlocking, it was not until 1904 that plans were agreed at an estimated cost of £11,000 for the resignalling at Keith. The new Keith Junction cabin, which is still in use, was finally opened on 9th October 1905, at which time Newmill and Keith Ground Frame were closed. A subsidiary cabin, known as Keith North, was built on the Dufftown platform to control the points at that end of the station.

However, the short single line through the station between GNSR and Highland boxes remained worked by telephone until 1966, the only protection for trains being through the interlocking of the signals controlling entry to the through platform.

On the Dufftown line, electric tablet working was introduced on 25th July 1892 between Drummuir and Dufftown using Tyers No.4a instruments. Then on 31st December 1895 a new loop together with North and South signal boxes and interlocked points and signals was brought into use at Auchindachy, together with tablet working to Drummuir. At the latter, interlocked signalling from East and West signal boxes was brought into use on 8th January 1894 at noon. Dufftown was resignalled with North and South boxes on 17th September 1894. It is not know when tablet working was introduced to Craigellachie, but it was not until 10th December 1900 that the three new signal boxes there were brought into use. There were repeated letters from the Board of Trade to the GNSR during the late 1890s demanding that action be taken to provide interlocked signalling; the Great North's stalling tactics did allow it to phase the necessary expenditure.

As the gradient out of Dufftown towards Drummuir was steep, goods trains could be banked up the hill. A

A curious signal at Keith was the up Dufftown line home, which also supported the telegraph wires. The right hand bracket controlled access to the loop and allowed goods trains to enter the yard when the platform was occupied. (LGRP)

separate Banking Key was issued at Dufftown to the driver of the banking engine to enable the banker to return to Dufftown. This was interlocked with the single line token and had to be returned to Dufftown before another train was allowed in the section.

During the late 1920s, the tablet instruments were replaced by Tyer's Key Token. Auchindachy loop was not needed throughout the day, so as an economy measure, long section working was introduced between Drummuir and Keith on 23rd August 1931. The North box at Auchindachy was dispensed with and the up home replaced by a junction signal so that up trains could use the down platform. When the South box was closed, the long section token could be used to give access to the sidings. Auchindachy loop was taken out of use on 1st September 1964 and the loop closed while the same happened at Drummuir on 16th July 1966. The two boxes at Dufftown survived until 15th December 1968, some months after the passenger closure, and a ground frame was then provided to control access to the sidings. The three boxes at Craigellachie were taken out of use on 15th December 1968. One engine in steam operation was then introduced.

During 1966, all the intermediate signal boxes between Keith and Elgin were closed. The two Highland signal boxes at Keith were closed on 23rd October 1966 and all the points and sidings removed. The single line then extended from the GNSR cabin at Keith to Elgin. When the line east of Keith was singled, tokenless block working was introduced through Keith to Elgin. There was a scheme to replace this with Radio signalling in the late 1980s, but this was abandoned when it was realised that it could not handle the traffic. Since then, little has changed, although the signal boxes have been improved with better insulation and heating, giving signallers much more comfortable working conditions.

LMS economy - a Caledonian pattern signal arm mounted on a post made of old rail at the west end of the station still in use in January 1965. (Keith Fenwick)

(Right) There was room to spare at the Highland end of the station for a signal box but this elevated design atop the siding into the goods shed was chosen. It did give the signalman a commanding view of the tracks. Photographed in May 1952. The box had a Dutton style frame.　　　　　　　　　　*(J L Stevenson)*

A southbound train leaving Keith in the 1950s. This would join a Coast portion at Cairnie. The loco is a Class K2, originally built for the Great Northern Railway. Several were transferred to Scotland in the 1920s particularly to work the West Highland line. Nine of the class came to the GNSR section in the 1950s after they had been replaced by more modern motive power further south. Definitely a case of cascading.

(W A A Bremner)

Class B1 No.61347 on the 3.45pm Aberdeen to Elgin via Dufftown on 15th August 1959. This served most stations from Aberdeen, reaching Keith at 5.40pm. It left at 5.45 and arrived at Elgin at 6.51pm.

(Douglas Hume)

Train Services

The general pattern of early train services is illustrated in the timetables already reproduced with trains serving all stations. Although the pace of travel was leisurely, this did not ensure that connections were maintained as delays on single lines had a knock-on effect so each company tried to keep independently to its own timetable.

The main northbound service from Aberdeen left in late afternoon (4.40pm in 1863) in connection with the departure from London Euston at 9pm the previous evening. This conveyed mails and therefore a connection had to be kept at Aberdeen but the train from the south was often late. As early as 1859, there was a complaint from a passenger who missed his connection for Elgin in Aberdeen and had to spend the night at Keith. The inconvenience and unreliability of connections at Aberdeen and Keith was one of the arguments used in favour of building the direct line to Perth from Inverness. After that opened, passengers between Elgin and Inverness faced further delays at Forres waiting for trains from Perth. The problem does not seem to have gone away. In 1903, it was recorded that from 1st August to 9th October, the 3.35pm train from Inverness was late at Keith necessitating duplication of the connecting train to Aberdeen on 25 out of 60 days.

Returning to the 1860s, the mails were speeded up from the south and transferred to the early afternoon train, but the Great North saw no need to accelerate its service. The opening of the Joint station at Aberdeen in 1867 was a great help to through passengers. In those days, there were also two overnight and one daytime goods trains and the mid-morning train ran as mixed.

Twenty years later, the stopping trains ran at roughly the same times, but there were now three extra fast trains, at 3.55am, 10.10am and 3.35pm from Aberdeen, and the service catered for the Coast route. The express trains split at Huntly but the other trains ran to Keith, with connections there to Coast line trains. Highland connections at Keith were patchy; the 10.10am express reached Elgin via both Dufftown and the Coast before the Highland train from Keith. At this time, none of the timetables show the availability of through coaches between Aberdeen and Inverness, so it is not clear if passengers had to change trains. The Great North certainly gave Elgin passengers a more convenient service to Aberdeen.

In 1897, the long-running feud between the Highland and Great North over transfer of traffic at Elgin was settled and a lavish service provided of eight through trains per day, soon reduced to six to match the traffic on offer. The timetable for June 1901 shows a remarkable similarity to that for 15 years earlier, although trains were faster and now split at Cairnie. Passengers from Keith to Portsoy and Banff also generally changed there. The main addition was a late through train from Aberdeen at 6.45pm reaching Elgin at 9.5pm. On slower services it could still take 2 hours to reach Keith from Aberdeen.

The First World War saw a severe curtailment of train services nationally, especially in 1917 when through passengers between Aberdeen and Inverness had to spend hours waiting at Keith. By the Grouping in 1923, services were back to normal but still similar to what was offered 25 years before. The main morning train from Aberdeen, at 8.5am and in connection with sleepers from the south, now conveyed a restaurant car which ran through to Inverness via Dufftown and returned on the 12.50pm from Inverness to serve lunch. Another interesting

BR Class 4 No.76107 storms out of Keith on the 3.55pm Aberdeen to Elgin via Dufftown on 13th May 1961, just before the end of steam. The coaches are Stanier designed LMS vehicles.   (Photo Douglas Hume)

development in 1923 was the introduction of through sleeping cars between London and Elgin and Lossiemouth during the summer months, running via Dufftown in both directions. For the first year, they were provided via both East and West Coast routes, although the Euston sleeper ran only for part of the first season and never operated again.

The LNER and LMS made changes to reflect the growth in longer distance traffic and the decline in local journeys. An erratic pattern of serving the quieter stations developed which continued until the closures of the 1960s. This enabled journey times for the majority to be improved. It had always been the practice at holiday times to run strengthened trains and often to run the separate portions independently south of Cairnie. Towards the end of the 1930s, this became more established. For instance, in 1938 the main morning service from Aberdeen started with a local at 7.5am. This was overtaken by the 7.50am at Huntly, conveying through coaches and restaurant car to Inverness and a sleeping car from London to Lossiemouth, and running non stop thence to Keith Town. A second fast train left Aberdeen at 8.5am with portions for both Coast and Glen routes, the latter again serving Keith Town only. On Saturdays there was a through train from Edinburgh to Elgin via Dufftown, replacing through carriages attached to the 2.20pm train on other days of the week.

Excursion traffic had always been important, but in the 1930s it became more established. The LNER put on a Thursday only train in the summer leaving Aberdeen at 11.50am and reaching Inverness at 3.5pm, the fastest time until then. A restaurant car was included in this train which stopped only at Huntly, Keith, Elgin, Forres and Nairn.

Sunday trains were never operated by the GNSR, but the LNER did start operating some in the summer. It was not until 8th April 1979 that they became a year-round facility.

The early years of British Railways were marked by retrenchment. In the early 1950s, it was

One of the unsuccessful innovations of the modernisation plan were the 4-wheeled diesel railbuses. At first, they attracted traffic but in time they proved to be unreliable and uncomfortable on longer journeys. The Speyside line was one of the first converted and allowed some trains to run through to Keith. After working up from Aviemore, this is the 09.40 return working in October 1964.

(Douglas Hume)

coal shortages which caused severe reductions in services and these were only slowly restored to something like previous levels. Some stations were now very poorly, and quite illogically, served. In 1958, Auchindachy was served by only one train from Keith but three in the other direction. The last train of the day from Keith to Dufftown left Aberdeen at 3.45pm and Keith at 5.45pm; it could still take 2 hours to reach Keith from Aberdeen.

In 1960, an experimental fast through train was introduced twice a day each way between Aberdeen and Inverness, completing the journey in 2½ hours with limited stops; initially it was non-stop between Aberdeen and Keith. This was such a success that the initial 3 month trial was made permanent and the service increased to 4 each way the following year, with some trains also serving Huntly. The rest of the service was re-organised around these trains. Since there was now a mixture of diesel multiple units and loco hauled trains, fewer trains split at Cairnie or Keith; instead passengers had to change trains.

After the closures took place in 1968, the service pattern was standardised on through trains between Aberdeen and Inverness. Frequency has been gradually increased so that there are now eleven trains daily and five on Sundays through Keith. At times, there have been workings from Aberdeen which terminated at Keith using the bay platform, but that is no longer the practice, although the platform remains available for use except during darkness as it has no lighting.

This Class 25 was typical of the diesels which worked freight services after dieselisation and then took over passenger workings in the late 1970s. Here No.25 245 shunts at Keith.

(Graham Maxtone collection)

Shunting in full swing at Keith on 2nd June 1960. The loco is ex-North British Railway Class N15 No.69224 which by then had been nominally transferred from Keith to Ferryhill. (Photo Douglas Hume)

The SRPS has organised many tours throughout Scotland over the last 40 years using their own coaches, which include several of historic interest. This is the Fife Coast Express which visited Dufftown behind a class 40 in May 1978. The leading vehicle is the ex-GNSR Royal Saloon which was used after 1923 as an Inspection Saloon. The SRPS rescued it in 1965. The bay platforms were once in the overgrown area in the foreground. (Mike Cooper)

Recollections of Life on the Railway 1962 - 1998

Ian Hird writes about his time at Keith.

"I started working on the Railway in 1962, just when steam had all but disappeared and diesels were being used on nearly all services. I was employed as Goods Porter relief (temporary summer). My home station was Keith. One of my first jobs was assisting loading whisky at Parkmore siding in Dufftown. This was done into open wagons (hyfits) with the casks being stood on their ends on the floor, and, if not a full wagon, the casks had to be roped to stop them moving in transit. Other jobs included assisting at the very busy freight sheds at Keith and Huntly, which served the towns and the surrounding area, and at various stations around the north east such as Craigellachie, Aberlour, Elgin, etc.

"After four months I progressed to a permanent post at Keith as Goods Porter. I spent six months at this post, loading coal on a daily basis by 'shovel' from mineral wagons to a small lorry primarily for Glen Keith distillery and other distilleries in the area. No sooner had the coal wagons been emptied and caught up on, with maybe one left, then another dozen would be placed in the siding to start all over again. Around 20 wagons of coal per week came in, all for unloading by 'shovel' to a lorry for delivery to local distilleries. In the Goods shed other arduous tasks included unloading grain from open wagons to lorries, usually sheeted against the weather, for local delivery. Bags were 2 cwt. (224 lbs.) made of very rough Hessian which made you go home tired, saddle sore and hungry. Another job to be disliked was unloading of 'basic slag' in little bags, which felt like they were nailed to the floor. All manner of goods was handled by the railway and you never knew what would crop up next.

"I moved on to a job in Keith freight yard as Coupler on permanent 1400 to 2200 shift Mondays to Fridays. My job was to couple on the wagons as trains were made up and generally assist the Shunter and Head Shunter. Tools of the trade were a shunting pole which, if it was a good one, you guarded with your life, and a paraffin handlamp, with red, green and clear aspects, which was polished to perfection. This lamp could be your life saver in the dark so it was very important to look after it.

"Lots of the couplings were simple link couplings, e.g. on coal wagons, but more and more wagons were being introduced with screw or instanter couplings and fitted brakes. It was not uncommon to have trains of two engines and 75 standard wagon lengths leaving Keith for the north and the south. This was the maximum length allowed for crossing purposes at other stations.

"Keith yard was manned 24 hours per day Monday to Saturday with 3 shifts i.e. 00.01 to 08.00, 08.00 to 16.00 and 16.00 to 24.00. A typical freight timetable for a morning around the year 1965 went like this:-

Freight from previous back shift which had not been sorted, notably livestock from sales at Dingwall and the North, to be shunted.

01.30 - Arrival of freight from Aberdeen

03.00 - Arrival of 'Hielan Piper' (70 mph Express) fully fitted freight to the North for attach and detach. This was a brave experiment by British Railways in the 1950s to improve goods transit times and ran from Glasgow to Inverness via Aberdeen. There was no corresponding up train, reflecting the nature of the traffic it carried.

By May 1989, when this view of Keith looking towards the Dufftown platform was taken, very little traffic remained in the goods yard. A grain wagon on the right and in the distance a bulk tanker for whisky and a flat wagon are the only vehicles visible. The track which had been lifted was originally connected at the Dufftown end to the running line to give freight trains from the Dufftown line direct access to the goods yard; it was later relaid.   *(Keith Fenwick)*

04.30 - Arrival of loose coupled freight from Aberdeen for North. Attach engine and usually around 20 to 30 wagons. Train normally 50 to 70 wagon lengths on departure.

05.20 - Departure of early Coast freight. Brake-van on each end to assist rounding at Cairnie Junction.

06.20 - Departure of Speyside freight via Dufftown, Craigellachie and on to Aviemore.

06.30 - Arrival of Passenger. Detach newspaper vans and horseboxes of calves daily.

07.05 - Arrival of freight from Aberdeen.

09.30 - Departure of late Coast freight.

10.15 - Arrival of freight from North.

10.30 - Departure of North freight via Elgin.

12.30 - Departure of freight to Aberdeen, normally empties.

13.40 - Departure of second Speyside freight.

"Shunting pilots at Keith were a Barclay 204 h.p. and latterly an English Electric 350 h.p. After the pilots were withdrawn shunting was done by English Electric 1000's (Class 20) or anything that was available which sometimes was a MAN (NB Type 2), class 24 or 26 or even a class 40. These large engines were not very suitable for yard shunting. The 'puggy' was the ideal machine for the job.

"Sidings at Keith yard with capacity in standard wagon lengths were - Shed road (through the Goods shed, 35 wagons), Highland road (10 wagons), New road (for unloading, 28 wagons), Middle road (35 wagons), Bank (also for unloading, 38 wagons), Horsebox (for unloading calves etc., 3 wagons), No.5 (30 wagons), No.4 (25 wagons), No.3 (39 wagons) and No.2 (the acceptance siding for freight trains, with rounding facility, 35 wagons). Siding No.1 gave access to loco sidings and loco shed. The 'Tattie Road', which was the back shunt, had a capacity of around 75 wagons.

"Most trains were accepted either in No 2 siding or on the 'Back road' with rounding via Kynoch's Gates. It was not uncommon for trains to be lying back at Cairnie, Drummuir, Elgin or sitting round at the 'Hielan' waiting to get into the Keith yard. 'Fair across' was the common cry to the Signalman which meant no more trains could be accepted until the yard was cleared by a train departure or storage down the 'Tattie Road'.

"The busiest shift was always a Tuesday back shift (16.00 to 24.00). Every Tuesday probably on average around 80 to 100 wagons of whisky would arrive between the latter part of the day shift and the back shift. This was over and above the other normal traffic. All had to be shunted according to destination, normally to the south. Every Tuesday night a booked service of whisky only, comprising of 45 wagons, would leave No 3 siding at 21.15 for the south. This train was a fully fitted service with every vehicle braked. This followed the normal freight service at 20.53 also for the south which would have a 'fitted head' of whisky. This combined with the potato season meant not much rest for the shunters etc.

"Perhaps I should give an explanation of 'fitted head'. This referred to fully braked wagons marshalled at the head of the train to provide extra brake force and enable the train to run faster. There were tables of loads allowed with specific engines on a specific route which showed how many fitted wagons were required. If not enough fitted vehicles were run in the train, it was operated at a lower speed, usually 25 m.p.h.

"Also worth a mention was trip working to the local distilleries. There were three trips per day. One trip ran to Aultmore distillery, up what was left of the old Buckie line. It was only allowed 10 vehicles and brake van propelling, meaning the engine was on the rear, because no facilities existed to round the train at Aultmore. Another trip ran to Glentauchers distillery and was locked into the siding off the Main line. The third trip ran to Strathmill distillery and was also locked into the siding. In addition, every day there were trips round to the 'Hielan' to shunt Kynoch's and J.L.Hay coal sidings. And passenger trains were running as well. How did we manage?

"Other duties were strengthening passenger trains by attaching extra coaches on local holidays etc. and maybe attaching vans of yeast for distillery use to Speyside passenger trains. A very busy place was Keith freight yard in the 1960's as were most yards all over the system.

A Freightliner container is backed up against the through platform for loading in August 1970. This was a time when container traffic was seen as a major growth area, but it is not clear what traffic was being carried here.

(Photo Norris Forrest)

"I progressed to Shunter which meant you were responsible for all the sets of hand operated points in Keith yard and you took your orders from the Head Shunter. Further progress some months later allowed me to advance to Head Shunter. This post meant you were responsible for all shunting operations and I had to answer to the Station Master who at that time was a certain R. Mackenzie (now deceased). A very fair man who ruled all operations at the station with a 'rod of iron' and dare I mention a little swearing.

"I moved on to other duties, being made redundant when the Coast line closed in 1968 and became a lorry driver but still with B.R. then in turn National Carriers. This involved coal and other goods deliveries all round the coast, notably the light bulb factory at Buckie who got a fair amount of traffic. I moved on to be a freight guard with some passenger guard duties after the coast deliveries dried up and worked some of the last freight runs to Dufftown with coal and grain. I also acted as conductor, assisting a guard who was not signed for the branch, on the West Highlander charter which used to go to Dufftown as part of its excursion.

"Sadly the 'Beeching' cuts sent us into decline and with the Coast line shut, plus most of the branch lines also shut, the freight eventually disappeared onto the road leaving a surplus staff, empty goods yards and disused rolling stock and engines. When I started on the railways in 1962 there was around 100 staff employed at Keith between drivers, firemen, signalmen, permanent way gangs and station staff. Today you could count all the staff on one hand. Progress - I don't think so.

"I thoroughly enjoyed my career on the railways and the 'crack' and the fun with all the pranks was great. Many a derailment in the yard was sorted out without any fuss. All this is all gone and just wonderful distant memories.

"I eventually finished up in the Ticket Office in the new station at Keith, all by myself, and took early retirement, leaving in 1998 after 35 years service."

In May 2009, the first Royal Scotsman of the season was backed into the Dufftown platform at Keith by 47787 Windsor Castle. *The Chivas Regal plant is behind the train.* (Ron Smith)

Dufftown Line Revival

When British Rail decided to abandon the railway line between Keith and Dufftown, the first proposal was to convert the 11 miles into a public walkway. Local feeling was against the track being torn up. The line had already demonstrated that it could attract visitors to the area, so why should this valuable resource be lost? Clearly only voluntary local effort could achieve anything. A meeting in Keith in September 1992 formed a Steering Group chaired by Keith solicitor Ray Sneddon, and an alternative strategy to save the line as a tourist attraction was put forward. The Keith & Dufftown Railway Association was launched at a meeting in Keith on 17th June 1993.

The new strategy was based on "steam" and "tourism", and the concept of a Victorian "corridor" between the two towns, linking the heritage of castles, churches, Victorian industry and distilleries. The first major hurdles were to raise an estimated £60,000 to repair the Fiddich Viaduct at Dufftown and to open negotiations with British Rail. KDRA offered to purchase the line from Dufftown to Keith Town for a nominal sum in return for taking over all liabilities and being given access to the Keith Junction platform, engine shed, yard, turning facilities and main line access.

After a lot of effort, funding of £5,150 was secured for the structural survey of the Fiddich Viaduct and British Rail granted an initial 18 month lease on Dufftown Station, which allowed building restoration to commence. By April 1994 Grampian Regional Council had confirmed that the Fiddich Viaduct was structurally sound, but needed some restoration, and that there were no major problems with the other bridges and culverts.

By mid-1994 KDRA were dealing with the British Rail Property Board and the newly formed Railtrack, which complicated matters somewhat. A major breakthrough was announced in July

One of the first projects undertaken by the KDRA was the restoration of Dufftown station building to demonstrate confidence in the project. The interior was adapted to its new role but retains many original features, as does the outside. This was its condition in June 2000. Since then, the harling has caused problems and has been removed to expose the stonework, with repointing to ensure durability. *(Keith Fenwick)*

with funding for the Fiddich Viaduct repairs confirmed by Highlands & Islands Enterprise, to be carried out over 3 years from April 1995. This news also allowed the Association to form the Keith & Dufftown Railway Company, to proceed with the purchase of the line at a cost of £1 per mile (total £11), and to apply for a Light Railway Order to operate the railway.

However, 1995 came and went with the purchase negotiations dragging on. Railtrack became "tight lipped" about the future of Keith Junction yard and this threw some doubt on the future ability of KDRA trains to access and "run round". On a more positive note, BR allowed Morrison Construction to start repair work on Fiddich Viaduct in June, despite transfer of line ownership not being settled. Volunteers continued to work at Dufftown on the station building, permanent way clearance and fencing and one or two items of rolling stock were delivered. Additional European funding of £84,000 was secured for the section from the Fiddich Viaduct to Drummuir (in addition to the £60,000 for the Viaduct), but could not be used until ownership was secured. Funds were running low and severe flooding in September caused significant damage along the line.

In late 1997 the KDRA Board dropped a bombshell on its members. It appeared that not only would Railtrack not allow access into Keith Junction, they required up to £20,000 to effect a physical line disconnection (2 rail lengths) and the installation of buffers. The disconnection was to be "temporary" and the purchase of the line could not be completed without this action. It was also becoming apparent that the steam dream was fading and talk was turning towards diesel multiple units for the operation of public services, initially planned from Dufftown to Loch Park. European Rural Development Funding of £288,000 had now been secured, of which £115,000 was for the Fiddich Viaduct and £27,000 for the refurbishment of Dufftown Station. It was anticipated that bridge and structure repairs from Dufftown to Loch Park would need a further £70,000 and track repair another £25,000. The cost of rebuilding Keith Town Station was estimated at £85,000. Anticipated completion of all line work was now 2000.

Coincidental to the disconnection and following an approach from the North of Scotland Water Authority, the Association agreed to lift a further 13 panels of track between Keith Junction and Keith Town in December 1998 to allow the installation of a new sewer system. In return the Water Authority paid £38,000 to the Association. It was intended to relay the track after project completion in late 1999, but this has never happened. On Thursday 27th August

Clayton 0-4-0 diesel mechanical shunter The Wee Mac *was the first locomotive to arrive on the railway. It was built in 1979 and was first used at the Royal Naval Dockyard in Rosyth, Fife. After a short career there, it was purchased by the Macallan Distillery who kindly gifted it to the Railway in 1994. It was used extensively during the line's restoration.*
Keith Fenwick

The upstairs part of the new station building at Keith Town. An internal stair leads to the main building below. The complete building is illustrated on page 65.

(Keith Fenwick)

1998 the Dufftown line was disconnected from the railway network. This made the K&DR the longest preserved railway in Scotland and most northerly in Britain and, more importantly, allowed the purchase and Light Railway Order application to be progressed. There was an interesting footnote to the Light Railway Order application – only one objection was received and, incredibly, it came from Railtrack, who later withdrew it!

As 1999 progressed line clearance and repair work was stepped up as the railway anticipated inspection by Her Majesty's Railway Inspector. The Rule Book was now in place and this allowed a Works Train to operate. It also allowed operator training to start. The local M.P., Margaret Ewing, and the M.E.P, Winnie Ewing, lobbied on behalf of the Association and took the issue of the Light Railway Order to the Deputy Prime Minister, John Prescott. The Order was signed on 20th July 1999 and this (and the disconnection from the main rail system) allowed the Association to conclude the bargain for the purchase of the railway with Rail Property Ltd (formerly British Rail Property Board).

By the end of the year European funding was in place for the Loch Park to Keith Town section, including the rebuilding of Keith Town Station and car park. The projected funding for this phase was £457,000.

In early 2000 the railway was dealing with Major Poyntz of Her Majesty's Railway Inspectorate, with the inspection visit scheduled for May and line operations starting thereafter. In January another setback occurred, however, when Hastings Diesels suddenly withdrew their offer to hire a DEMU. Suddenly, the railway found itself almost ready to open, but with no train! Thankfully, the Railcar Association and Diesel Unit Preservation Associates Limited came to the rescue and provided a Class 108 DMU after much frantic negotiation. Finally, on 3rd June 2000, after 8 long years, the first KDRA train departed Dufftown for Drummuir, although still not able to call there. Platform repairs were completed on 6th July and two days later, the line was officially re-opened by Councillor Eddie Aldridge, Convener of Moray Council, which had stood firmly behind the Association.

One year later, on Saturday 18th August 2001, the first KDRA train to run over the entire 11 mile line pulled into Keith Town. The late John Begg, Managing Director of Grampian Rail Tours, performed the opening ceremony at Dufftown and "baptised" the newly named *Spirit of Banffshire* dmu with a dram. When the train arrived at Keith Town well-wishers were thronging the road bridges and station to greet the return of an old friend. The Keith & Dufftown railway had been saved.

Today the railway operates as The Whisky Line on Saturdays and Sundays from Easter to the end of September plus Fridays in June, July and August. Special events are held throughout the year, including Santa Trains in December. There have been many improvements along the line. At Keith Town, new wooden buildings have been erected in the style of those which once stood there; an exact replica was not feasible to meet current standards.

Nothing remained at Drummuir when the KDRA took over. The platform has been rebuilt and it is hoped one day to erect a building on it. Several changes had taken place at Dufftown, the operating base of the railway. The 1960s grain silos have gone and the sidings are used for storage. A new two-road shed has been built at the Craigellachie end of the station to provide covered storage and workshop accommodation. One of the earliest jobs undertaken was the restoration of the station building. As well as the booking office and shop, a display of historical material has been set up. Along the platform, a couple of converted Mark 1 coaches provide for the culinary needs of visitors with some excellent home-cooking. Parties can also be catered for in an ex-Mark 2 second open coach. A couple of ex-Brighton Belle Pullman coaches did provide this facility, but they have returned south for restoration and possible main line use.

The first locomotive on the railway was a four wheel Clayton shunter built in 1979, gifted by Macallan Distillery. It carries the Macallan livery and is known by the name of *Wee Mac*. In March 2000 *Wee Mac* was joined by *Spirit O'Fife*, an 0-6-0 diesel mechanical shunter built for the Seaham Dock Company in 1967 by English Electric. It carried serial number D1193 to allow it to operate on British Railway freight exchange sidings at the docks. Following the closure of rail operations at Seaham, it was sold to Scottish Grain Distillers (now part of Diageo) at Cameron Bridge Distillery in Fife. After rail traffic ceased in 1998, the locomotive came to Dufftown in March 2000 on long-term loan. Other rolling stock includes the unique two-coach class 140 railbus built in 1981. Passenger services are provided by 2 two-coach class 108 diesel multiple units, one named *Spirit of Speyside* and the other *Spirit of Banffshire*. There is also one other coach from a class 108 unit together with several wagons for works train use.

Dufftown in June 2000 was the scene of much activity. The platform, which had been cut back when the second grain silo was built, was being extended again. In effect the single wagon load/ sundries part of the yard had been moved over to accommodate the four grain sidings. By that time the shorter trains could easily be accommodated. The rebuilt platform was widened to serve the siding on the right where the buffet cars are now located.
(Keith Fenwick)

The Future

The Aberdeen to Inverness railway line continues to provide a very necessary public service, although only courtesy of a generous public subsidy, and is now an integral part of ScotRail's network. It provides a much more comfortable journey from places such as Keith and Elgin than the parallel A96. Demand has grown over the last 20 years and ways of improving both speed and frequency have been proposed.

In June 2012 the Scottish Government announced phase one of the Aberdeen to Inverness Rail Improvement Project to be financed and delivered in partnership with Network Rail during the five year period 2014 to 2019. This will see capacity improvements and new stations at Kintore and Dalcross. From March 2015, ScotRail services will be subject to a new franchise agreement; whether operations remain with Firstgroup or pass to another company will depend on the assessment of tenders by Transport Scotland.

No freight trains are currently timetabled north of Aberdeen, although the route as far as Elgin was cleared for larger containers in 2007. However, the route is used for traffic diverted from the Highland main line if that is not available. Opportunities remain to originate freight in the locality, particularly to serve the whisky industry.

The Keith & Dufftown Railway is now well-established as a tourist attraction in the area. Maintaining and enhancing such a service when operated entirely by volunteers is no mean feat. Maybe one day it will be possible to restore the link to the Junction station at Keith but for the majority of passengers the terminus near the middle of the town is very convenient.

Nobody can tell what will happen in the future, but there is every reason to believe that the line opened over 150 years ago will continue to provide an essential service to Keith and the surrounding area for many years to come.

The 1988-built station at Keith is light and airy, photographed in 2006. The porch on the platform side was added when the awning over the platform was removed in 1998. (Keith Fenwick)

The Great North of Scotland Railway Association caters for all those interested in the history of the Great North of Scotland Railway and its constituent companies, as well as the LNER, British Railways and ScotRail periods. It facilitates and co-ordinates members' research and provides information for modellers.

Members receive a quarterly *Review* containing articles, photographs, drawings and news of the railway, both historical and current. The Association has published a number of books which members can purchase at a discount. A large archive of documents, drawings and photographs has been built up which is of particular value to modellers. Meetings and excursions are regularly organised for the benefit of members. For further information, please have a look at the Association's website :

www.gnsra.org.uk.

The Highland Railway Society brings together all those interested in the Highland Railway, its predecessors and successors. An illustrated quarterly *Journal* is published by the Society giving a wide variety of articles and enabling members to exchange information and opinions. Several books have been published by the Society to complement those available commercially. The Society has Library, Photographic and Drawing collections which are enhanced regularly and are available to members. Copies of drawings are available for purchase by members. A collection of small artefacts has also been built up. Modellers' needs are given particular attention. More information about the Society can be obtained on the Society's web site :

www.hrsoc.org.uk.

The Keith & Dufftown Railway Association, formed in 1993, operates "The Whisky Line" - the most northerly heritage railway in the United Kingdom. The 11 mile line links the two whisky towns of Keith and Dufftown and the Association maintains and develops the railway services and facilities. The Association is run entirely by a small group of dedicated volunteers, with work ranging from train operational duties, non-operational roles (e.g. engineering, joinery, painting, etc.) and back-up support (e.g. catering, booking office, the shop, etc.). Trains run on Saturday and Sunday in April (from Easter), May and September and on Friday, Saturday and Sunday in June, July and August. There are a number of special events throughout the year.

We are always looking for enthusiastic volunteers with a variety of skills. If you are interested in joining or supporting the Association, please write to KDRA, Dufftown Station, Dufftown, Banffshire, AB55 4BA; or telephone 01340 821181 (Tuesday & operational days only). You will be assured of a warm welcome. The latest information can be found on our website :

www.keith-dufftown-railway.co.uk;

Rear Cover

Upper : Today's services are mainly provided by Class 158 two-car diesel units, which date from 1989-1992 and are used throughout Great Britain. A four-coach train, in First ScotRail livery and maintained in spotless condition by Inverness depot, approaches Keith in June 2008 past the site of the turntable.   (Ron Smith)

Lower : An exciting development in 2012 was the first operation of steam over the KDR since 1961. A special weekend was organised to celebrate the 150th anniversary of the opening of the line and Class 2 No.46512 was hired from the Strathspey Railway to work the trains. Since there was no run-round facility at Keith Town, a shunter and Strathmill Distillery siding were used to get the loco to the other end of the train. Here a Keith-bound train tackles the 1 in 60 climb from Parkmore towards Loch Park on 14th October 2012.

(David Purser)